When Daisy met Tommy

The story of a little girl and her adopted brother

WITHDRAWN

JULES BELLE

Published by
British Association for Adoption & Fostering
(BAAF)
Saffron House
6–10 Kirby Street
London EC1N 8TS
www.baaf.org.uk

Charity registration 275689 (England & Wales)
and SC039337 (Scotland)

British Library Cataloguing in Publication Data
A catalogue record for this book is available from
the British Library

ISBN 978 1 907585 06 7

Project management by Abi Omotoso, BAAF
Photograph on cover posed by models, by istockphoto.com
Designed by Helen Joubert Designs
Typeset by Fravashi Aga
Printed in Great Britain by TJ International
Trade distribution by Turnaround Publisher Services, Unit 3,
Olympia Trading Estate, Coburg Road, London N22 6TZ

BAAF is the leading UK-wide membership organisation for all
those concerned with adoption, fostering and child care issues.

The paper used for the text pages of this book is FSC certified.
FSC (Forest Stewardship Council) is an international network to
promote responsible management of the world's forests.

Printed on totally chlorine-free paper.

FSC
Mixed Sources
Product group from well-managed
forests and other controlled sources

Cert no. SGS-COC-2482
www.fsc.org
© 1996 Forest Stewardship Council

Contents

Acknowledgements

My three co-adventurers, my team mates: my family.

Einstein (get off my bed), the three musCATeers (I know which one of you stole the Delete key), Mum, Dad, and in order of size, my big brother and little sister. My in-laws (Sandra not least for all the Wednesdays), our extended family and friends. All for being yourselves.

Also Gill, sadly taken, adoptive mother of four, for taking the time at the very start of our adventure to tell us a few truths and some wonderful gems about the reality of adoption.

Our social workers for being top-notch; the foster carer and her son for loving ours; the birth mother of our boy without whom our home would be remarkably tidier and quieter to boot, but not nearly so perfect.

Hedi for believing this a worthy use of time, for your guidance, hard work and for all the red ink: I wear it well I think. Finally to BAAF, Shaila in particular, for publishing and Abi Omotoso for managing the project.

I owe you all a big thank you.

Names have been changed to protect the children's identity.

Note about the author

Jules is Southern by birth, was adopted by the Midlands at six and fostered by the North as a student. Aged nine, armed with her mother's typewriter, she hammered out a screenplay for eighties icon Michael J Fox. She has not looked back and has written ever since, most notably lists, and is working on her first novel.

In memory of baby Rémi

*And for Dorothy, the Scarecrow, the Tin Man
and the Cowardly Lion*

The Our Story series
This book is part of BAAF's Our Story series, which explores adoption and fostering experiences as told by adoptive parents and permanent foster carers.

The series editor
Hedi Argent is an independent family placement consultant, trainer and freelance writer. She is the author of *Find me a Family* (Souvenir Press, 1984), *Whatever Happened to Adam?* (BAAF, 1998), *Related by Adoption* (BAAF, 2004), *One of the Family* (BAAF, 2005), *Ten Top Tips for Placing Children in Families* (BAAF, 2006), *Josh and Jaz have Three Mums* (BAAF, 2007), *Ten Top Tips for Placing Siblings* (BAAF, 2008), and *Ten Top Tips for Supporting Kinship Placements* (BAAF, 2009). She is the co-author of *Taking Extra Care* (BAAF, 1997, with Ailee Kerrane) and *Dealing with Disruption* (BAAF, 2006, with Jeffrey Coleman), and the editor of *Keeping the Doors Open* (BAAF, 1988), *See You Soon* (BAAF, 1995), *Staying Connected* (BAAF, 2002), and *Models of Adoption Support* (BAAF, 2003). She has also written six illustrated booklets in the children's series published by BAAF: *What Happens in Court?* (2003, with Mary Lane), *What is Contact?* (2004), *What is a Disability?* (2004), *Life Story Work* (2005, with Shaila Shah), *What is Kinship Care?* (2007), and *Adopting a Brother or Sister* (2010).

1

Driving Miss Daisy where exactly?

'Tommy's really annoying,' is Daisy's favourite saying. But then she loves to say it, for she knows, you can hear it in her voice, that it is a luxury. The thing is, you see, it's not always just grown-ups who suffer from "baby bother". Daisy's "baby bother" began when she was only six months old in the form of an inexplicably, possibly prematurely broody mother. Now, more than six years later, there is what looks and sounds somewhat suspiciously like a baby boy competing to be the first to wake the household at 6am, who finds her toys infinitely more appealing than his own and who, give or take the occasional sibling scuffle, worships the ground that she, and she alone, walks on.

To an outsider he materialised magically, perhaps rather mysteriously, one winter's day last year. Like the chosen one. He descended on our home town with the not so distant promise of tinkling sleigh bells and in the wake of a rather intense high profile children's services case. The tragic death of a little boy, let down by the support systems around him, hung heavily in the air and played on the hearts and minds of the nation. Even in our little corner of the world, it was a very poignant time for Tom to arrive. Daisy was absolutely over the moon, unable to believe that she at long last had a brother, a baby one at that, and, if that wasn't already too much excitement to handle, just in time for Christmas. How magical that was. Oh yes, magical. I'll come back to that one later.

Of course it wasn't an immaculate conception and neither did he land unannounced on our doorstep one bright but cold morning. In fact, he had been hanging over Daisy for as long as she can remember. This book, this story, belongs to her: to her and to coin a phrase, Daisy's phrase, to her "baby bother". For ultimately she too had been dragged along for the ride; it was not just her parents who suffered the ball-breaking, exhausting heartache of second time infertility and survived the emotional rollercoaster and rigorous strains of the adoption process. At times we succeeded in protecting her whilst at others we fell far short of the mark, consequently exposing her to a very sobering grown-up world and one of impossible unknowns. Was it the right thing to do?

Today the answer is most emphatically yes. Tomorrow? I hope so with all my heart, but that is the leap of faith that we have taken as a family: the commitment that, come what may, we will make it work. For we embarked on this journey with an innocent bystander scooped up for the ride and there was no way we were about to let her down. Our eyes were wide open, hearts hopeful and minds wary but keen to learn so much more. A notoriously difficult avenue to travel, adoption comes with almost inevitable problems, and choosing to accept this is so very, very different from falling pregnant and dealing with the consequences. The literature and reference material available, and indeed the adoption agencies, make this crystal clear from the very beginning. For a grown-up it is a lot to consider. For a little girl just turning four years old, it was a minefield.

The knock-on effect of adoption for any existing children in a family is a most pressing issue requiring some considerable research and thought. It is perhaps a sign of the times that many, though not all, of the children waiting to be adopted are likely to have been taken by authorities from parents who have neglected them, often due to drink- and drug-related problems, rather than having been relinquished, as was more often the case in the past. In the age of the internet and mobile phone, there is the possibility of the birth family attempting unsuitable contact with an adopted child – particularly in cases where there is to be contact with birth siblings who themselves remain in contact, or indeed live with, birth family members. This could, in theory, have implications for all the existing children in a family; in real terms, for us that meant only one person: Daisy.

It is also important to take on board, when considering adoption, that the days of denial and secrecy are gone. Today's adopted children grow up knowing full well that they are adopted and appropriate contact with birth families, albeit more often than not in the form of letters, is usually promoted by adoption agencies. The impact of this link, this bond of both a positive and negative nature, should not be underestimated. Of course we had no way of knowing, when we set out, what our future contact arrangements would be.

If there seemed to be a reason not to adopt then Daisy was it. A parent's natural instinct is generally to protect their children, and how adoption might affect Daisy and any future child of ours was a serious consideration. If we were to proceed then two children's lives would change forever and we would be accountable for their happiness. So, was it the right thing to do? To be honest, nobody could answer that better than Daisy herself.

I'll introduce Daisy properly before we go any further.

Let's get one thing straight: my daughter may be pint-sized, about a foot smaller than all her friends, still waiting for any inkling of a wobbly tooth when all around her are becoming more than a little blasé about the nightly visits from the Tooth Fairy, and are as a result substantially better off financially, but she has the courage to walk amongst giants. She towers above many others in her understanding of the world, humbling me on a fairly regular basis, and of that I will be forever proud. Being pint-sized has failed to hold her down or curb her spirit. She has more attitude than you could swing your hips at, and it won't surprise you to hear that she doesn't mince her words: the green jumper I bought in the sales makes me look like a monster, the prime minister is not right for the job (quite frankly she preferred the last one) and I should absolutely never ever cut my hair short again. She's six almost seven now. She hasn't always been here though. There was a life before Daisy. There must have been for I remember giving birth to her.

I fell pregnant with Daisy almost immediately after I got broody. Once upon a time, for a fairy tale is what it seemed, I was one of them: a woman who decides to get pregnant and then proceeds to do so in the mere flutter of eyelashes. It was the autumn/winter of 2001 and there was something close to intoxicating in the air around James and me. Three hopeless but rather loveable moggies had helped to postpone the broodiness just long enough to get married and return from an idyllic, magical honeymoon in Sorrento, Italy. The terrifying events of September 11th brought us back to reality, a new reality, from which there was born an intense desire for the future we'd always dreamed of. As it happens, Daisy was born nine months to the day after she was conceived. She remained an only child for over six years. Though the threat, or promise, of a brother or sister was there almost as long.

For us, the realisation of the true extent of Daisy's

involvement in our baby-making saga started in a hospital waiting room with the words, 'You don't need another baby, you've got me,' said in that matter of fact, black is black and white is white way that a child does so well. Ouch. Well there it was; out of the mouths of babes, as they say. She looked at me squarely, unblinking, unflinching in her three-year-old knowledge. Yes, I thought, why was it we were still sat there? Had we really got nothing better to do with our lives? A timeshare in the local hospital's waiting room was hardly the family holiday we deserved and had long since needed.

Was now a good time to introduce the shades of grey that existed on the fringes of Daisy's black and white world? Dared we introduce the uncertainty that she was so far seemingly happily immune against? Or had the rot already set in? She waited unrelentingly for my response, which would, of course, allay all fears and arguments to the contrary. Wouldn't it? Now there's the thing.

I steeled myself, swallowed hard, wanting so badly to answer her the way she wanted me to. I shuffled in my plastic chair, adjusted her on my lap slightly and looked at James. He pulled a 'What do you say to that' face. To which I returned a 'Thanks for that, darling' look. She raised her eyebrows expectantly. I chewed my lip, breathing in as I did so, blew out and meant to say, 'Grab your coat and let's skedaddle,' or words to that effect. What I actually said I fail to recall. My mother would call it mumbling.

I looked at the clock again. An hour and a half behind time and when we did eventually walk out of here there would still be no baby. I would have nothing to show as justification. We'd brought her along to prevent her feeling left out; she had long since cottoned on to our countless mysterious trips to the hospital and I'd wanted to offer some humdrum reality to the mystery. Giving her a reassuring squeeze, I finally said the right thing, 'You're right. I don't. I don't need another baby.' But we stayed and the waiting continued and the uncertainty crept in. Quite obviously Mummy and Daddy didn't think she was enough. Quite obviously Mummy and Daddy did need another baby. Actions really do speak louder than words – ours undermined every last syllable.

It is a condition of parenthood to retire to bed feeling guilty about some terrible thing or other that you have or haven't said or done or thought. To lie awake worrying about the psychological scar you have left on your child that will, without a doubt, be the defining factor in their life. Again. That particular night I was racked with guilt. I've never been a selfish person. Was that still true? Was that what I was becoming? How much longer would I drag James and Daisy along with me on my quest for another baby? I knew one thing. One day, and soon, Daisy too would want me to give her a brother or sister. What if I couldn't?

I felt so very alone in my search for the answer and would take sanctuary in the bathroom hoping that the sound of the shower drowned out the sobs. Maybe it did or maybe it didn't. Either way, James and Daisy have been kind enough never to allude to these sessions of self-pity, if indeed they were aware of them. By this point, three years of unexplained infertility was taking its toll. I was only moving into my early thirties during this time and had always taken such good care of my health. Yet all around me women, some of them smoking and drinking, seemed to be getting pregnant, some accidentally, with their first and then their second child. And those not in the baby zone were blissfully confident that they would be able to tick that box at a time suitable to them.

Meanwhile, for us, the thing that was supposed to be life creating was soul destroying. It became obvious that it was high time to take that particular recreational activity off the curriculum and reinstate it as a hobby. We'd tried it all. Tried, not tried, pretended we were giving up, given up, fallen off the wagon, got back on again, gone holistic, gone ballistic, taken all the fertility drugs they could prescribe and had so much well meant interference that my body was no longer my own. This was not what it was supposed to be about. Had we lost sight of what we were aiming for here? A family. Our family. And didn't we already have that?

Daisy was to prove the most deciding of all the factors in our situation. Already having her made the possibility of adoption an even scarier and much riskier option than it would otherwise have been. I remember painfully one occasion, at a "stay and play" session I liked to take Daisy to, when I tried to defend my desire for another child, with some irony, to a mother of two. Still, she maintained she couldn't see why Daisy wouldn't be enough. Just as in the soulless waiting room at that hospital Daisy couldn't see why Daisy wouldn't be enough, and sitting there with her perched on my lap, or watching her sleep in her bed every night like an angel resting her wings, more beautiful than anything I've ever seen, neither could I.

The idea of adoption had filtered in and out of my life since I was a child; for James, however, not so: adoption was never going to happen; he couldn't ever see himself having someone else's child; how could he ever feel the same as he did about his perfect little girl? I wanted him to drive us forward, for someone else to be at the steering wheel. But at this point in time James was prepared, content even, for Daisy to be his only child. So would he stop us in our tracks? Would I let him? Did I love him enough to do so without resentment? Surely a daddy, Daisy's daddy, and my husband were more important than anything else? How could I even be thinking these things when we had her to consider?

Those dark moments still pass through my memory every so often. How could two people so much in love, and with Daisy to show for it, feel so far away from one another when all they ever wanted was to create a family? Quite obviously we were not ready to adopt. Besides, whilst there was no concrete explanation for our infertility there was still a chance, right? And it was that "chance" that continued to loom over Daisy for a good while yet.

Daisy was at nursery school, only months from starting school, and perhaps not quite so much my baby any more. Einstein, our lanky chocolate labrador retriever, who incidentally is great at snoring on sofas but utterly useless at retrieving, had very contentedly taken his rather hairy, distinctly smelly place in the family, offering a wonderfully gentle, if a little loopy, playmate for Daisy. 'He's my boy,' she says, 'my best friend.' He certainly helped heal some of our hurt. We were still persisting with fertility treatment, and miserable as hell with the perpetual ups and downs of it, but trying desperately not to lean on the outside world or to let it impede on what were, after all, Daisy's days. But something was changing.

It had become slowly clear that it was not the pregnancy we craved but a bigger family. This realisation for us was not a revolutionary moment, but a chain of feelings that had slowly linked together and were finally joined by the saddest moment of our lives to date.

We'd been waiting for news of my friends' first baby, and it was while we were getting up one morning, chatting excitedly with Daisy about the imminent new arrival, and getting her ready, that the phone rang. James answered it. Our friends' baby, a boy, had died during labour. All that expectation, all those hopes and dreams had gone in a devastating instant. Daisy sat on the sofa, quiet, staring at us while James and I just looked at one another. Tears streamed down my face, and I remember repeating, 'Oh my god, oh my god, oh my god.' We pulled ourselves together, attempted to explain it to Daisy without understanding it ourselves, and then ushered the poor child off to nursery school. The rest is not my story to tell.

The little boy's death did not change the way I felt. It did underline what I already knew and was instrumental in moving us forward. I believe to this day that you do not have to have seen your children to love them. I loved Daisy while she grew inside me, and Tom from the moment I heard about him. It is the first day at school, the cuddles, the little things that children say that make you laugh so heartily when they are finally, thankfully, in bed asleep, that we longed to repeat with our second child, not the biological link. It was James, interestingly enough, who made the call to stop the fertility treatment. We were reclaiming our lives. Enough was enough. Adoption was to be our choice, our option. We would set off down that road and see where our journey took us. We felt free at last and giddy with the power of decision.

Cue to the chat with Daisy. More of a fluffy chicks and buzzy bumblebees type of chat, suitable for four-year-olds, than the birds and bees one itself. I put all those jolly pregnant people we met to good use as case studies to show how, although all babies grow inside their mummy's tummy, not all the mummies are able to look after their children. 'Why?' was the inevitable question.

'Because…' I started thinking of all the material I had read, of the statistics, the facts and heart-wrenchingly gritty stories, 'because they might be too poorly or unhappy,' I continued, watching her every movement, thinking all the time of that proverbial can of worms. Daisy played coyly on the lounge floor, a question clearly forming. I decided to move quickly on to the point in hand rather than brave the wriggly worms.

'These children need new mummies and daddies.' I paused, wondering what her reaction, so absolutely crucial to us, would be. 'And most definitely new bossy big sisters,' I added. I saw her eyes flicker in recognition and so went for broke: 'Daddy and I were thinking that maybe we should give one of these children a home. That maybe we could be their new mummy and daddy and that you could be their big sister.'

Daisy is not the easiest girl to second-guess. She was still preoccupied with the startling fact that there were children out there without parents. When she realised we could do something about it, she turned round, matter of fact, and said: 'That's what we must do then,' quite obviously incredulous that we hadn't thought of it sooner. She did, however, have strict criteria: that they were to be younger and shorter than her and unable to do cartwheels. Over the time it took to get through the process, a mind blowing three years from beginning to end, Daisy's criteria changed to: a younger brother to make stink bombs with.

And so Daisy proudly announced our decision at the dinner table in her best friend's house, whose parents were privy to the news. 'We're adopting!' Her best friend, Holly, was mightily impressed, 'Wow, really?!' to which Daisy excitedly replied, 'Seriously!' Her beloved best friend then very politely, so as not to spoil the moment, asked, 'What's adopting?'

It proved to be a learning curve for a few people, young and old, at the infant school which Daisy now attended, and she would come home quite exasperated at having to explain it all at school yet again. Oh, the questions that we raised in those children's homes over the following years! A fabulous teacher helped by openly discussing and referring to adoption whenever there were baby announcements of which, naturally in Daisy's age group, there were plenty. Then, as luck would have it, a new boy joined their class, himself recently adopted, giving Daisy an anchor to refer back to. Her adopted brother or sister would be as normal as him, the same as any other child, despite the abnormal interest the very word "adoption" had seemed to stir up. Daisy says they have never discussed the matter together – both, I presume, just wanting to get on with the stuff of life. But she was no longer out there on her own.

'How was it on the playground sidelines?' I asked her today, and she said, 'I just wanted to be the same as everyone else.' The main thing she remembers feeling is annoyed because people just didn't understand and, what's more, it took such a long time and she had nothing to show for it for 'ages and ages'. Everyone else's new baby brothers and sisters put in their appearances pretty much according to the same plan. Our plan was a little left of centre and, what's more, some way out of sight around the corner. I know how she felt. There were so many earnest, genuinely interested enquiries, some quite breathtaking plain old nosiness, but there was still no news and still no child. I felt like a pregnant elephant in a travelling circus, at times disappearing off the radar only to return with the same old tricks and nothing new to satisfy the audience. Daisy's friends generally just lost interest in her invisible brother or sister and there were times when I think she did too, and who could blame her?

And so we three waded through unfamiliar territory, sticking together like mud. When the assessment finally began we continued waiting, all the while knowing, believing that we would be ready at just the right time to catch our child as she or he fell. And Daisy, now five years old, was holding out the biggest net going, for by this stage she had absolutely no intention of being an only child. Though her arms must have ached, for there was still more waiting. She took great delight in informing her impatient grandparents of the process. James' parents had originally hoped their second grandchild would be home for Christmas – the one shortly after we told them of our intention to adopt – and three Christmases later he was.

Daisy's reality was that the first years of her life, whilst full to the brim of fun, happiness and love, were overshadowed intermittently with confused, often fraught, sometimes struggling parents who knew just how damn lucky they were to have her, but couldn't fight a basic instinct to have another child and couldn't help but try. It is likely, thankfully, from chatting with Daisy, that our memory of this time is subjective, and that on balance we actually did a fair old job of being parents. Not that my dustbin kicking, feet stamping, rock star strops and sorry for myself sobbing sessions in the bathroom felt at all parent-like. In those early days I thought my body was letting me down, and worse still, I truly thought I was letting Daisy down. I've forgiven my body and myself. It's letting my children down that remains my greatest fear and therefore my motivation to get things right.

Daisy's recall of our infertility hell, however, is reassuringly non-existent. For her, the start of it all was adoption. She remembers everything about the adoption process and likes to re-examine random areas at will, 'Do you remember when we first met Tom at Cheryl's?' I do, it winds me up even now. Yet I am grateful that Daisy remembers the positives of that day, the 'This is my baby brother' moment.

I think I agree with Daisy. That really was the start of it all. Our adventure. The one-woman mission had evolved into something our little family was doing together. We truly were taking each step at a time on the understanding that we would get it right: we had to. We were adopting. Daisy was adopting. So I came straight out with it the other day when she was sitting near me watching television. 'Was it the right thing to do, Daisy?'

'What?' she asked, looking first at my laptop and then at me.

'Adopting Tom,' I said simply. I watched as she screwed her face up, shook her head slightly and, turning back to the television, pulled a despairing, confused and well practised face that they learn to do sometime after starting school.

'Course it was.' Then she shook her head again and sighed, raising her eyebrows, to reaffirm to the children's television presenter, I think, that Mum was officially mad and most definitely wasting her time. 'Jolly good,' said I.

And this is how, back in the saddle, James and I know we managed to get it right, which brings me to another equally important little person in all of this. There are, of course, two sides to every story and the many photos in our family home suggest Daisy is only half of the picture. There's somebody else you need to meet and he's not just any old Tom, Dick or Harry.

2

Tom, Dick or Harry

Meanwhile, a million miles away from where we were at, in what was actually only the other side of the same county, another altogether different story was being written. One quite unlike ours but so intrinsically entwined as to become a part of our story forever, and that, it has to be said, is a very, very long time whether young or old. Considering the extent of its significance to us, why then do we still really know so little of it? The answer is simple; with adoption you know what you are told. You are privileged only to know what the adoption agency knows. The rest is, could be, mere speculation: an educated guess at best.

So then, what do we know about the background of the little boy who was to become our son? Who, forgive me for being so blunt, could have been any old Tom, Dick or Harry. For though if asked outright, if probed on the subject, we will admit we do believe we were somehow always meant to be a family, so perfect is our match, the fact remains he simply was not always ours. Once upon a time he belonged to someone else. And that is a difficult story to have to tell him – perhaps an unwelcome intrusion into his healthy, rock solid sense of self and his sense of belonging. Difficult for both of our children for whom it will always remain something of a Brothers Grimm fairy tale. Though there is nothing fictitious about Tom.

If you were to meet Tom he'd introduce himself. The first thing you would notice is his silly grin, his baby soft curls and his dancing green eyes. Tom is one of life's winners; though only a toddler, you can see it straightaway. He draws others in and appears to charm effortlessly. Make no mistake, he is a rogue through and through and the rages he flies into are something else altogether; at times he manages to shock even himself. We attribute this to his strawberry blonde roots that glimmer with more than just the merest hint of red. Naturally, it should go without saying but I'll get it in anyway, the charismatic, charming, cute bits of Tom come from us. Not for the first or last time in our family does the infamous nature versus nurture debate raise its head.

Being as young as he is, Tom doesn't say much that we can decipher but what he does say is definite, to the point. There is no 'Mummy,' or 'Mamma,' but an unmistakable, definitive, almost proud, 'Mum,' which James says I respond to like the cat that got the cream. 'And why not?' for the truth is I waited a fair while to hear it and even now my chest swells just a little and I sigh inwardly with contentment. His earlier reluctance to use my "official title" may, of course, just be one of those things, or quite possibly it is attributable to the changes he endured in those formative early days: main carers who drifted in and out of his focus. Able to say 'Mamma,' from early on, he very rarely did, so very rarely reached out for me, wanting me only when ill and later for a short clingy patch on starting playgroup. Though very lucky when compared to most children in care, Tom had a painfully short time with his birth mother and a night alone in hospital with only the nurses to keep an eye on him, before having to adapt to a foster carer, and two weeks later spending a fortnight with the foster carer's mother before going back to the foster carer on her return from holiday. Then, after a few months of stability, he had keen old me to contend with. What was to say I wasn't going to disappear or simply fade out?

No, I don't mind admitting it, Tom was at first undeniably, perhaps understandably, drawn to any men in his life: James in particular. Something I found crushing at times considering the instrumental role I played in bringing him home to us, the hours I put into ensuring him a smooth transition into our lives, and yes, the love I was so keen to dish out. However, he's boy through and through and that is also something I was not used to. Tom's love comes as and when he feels like it – usually in passing en route to trouble – not unlike a lot of grown men I know.

Tom is in no rush to repeat on demand the few other words he does know – though the number is increasing daily – but babbles away to himself and anyone else who will listen all day, every day, pausing only to eat, sleep and identify every cat within a mile radius. He is a deft and determined climber though at one stage I swore blind he'd rather grow his fingernails and stretch than get up and crawl. He's obstinate, you see. Wilful. I'd love to claim that I have no idea where those particular attributes sit on the nature/nurture fence but I suspect he suffers here from a double dose from both his birth and adopted families. He has a silly sense of humour and despite being deemed not at all cuddly by his foster carer, he is in fact ridiculously so, and soppy to boot: when he chooses to be, of course. His two favourite possessions in the whole wide world, and I'm sure he'll thank me for this one day, are a rather unassuming teddy give to him by my parents, Alfie Bear, and a muslin square known as Snotrag, both of which he drags, Christopher Robin style, around with him whilst attempting death-defying feats that tend to end in tears and a need for yet more cuddles.

I can see many of his birth mother Sarah's features in him and hope very much that she gets to see them too one day. It is Sarah who holds the key to Tom's "family before us" history. This in itself is a slightly remarkable situation, with Tom being one of the very few healthy babies in the United Kingdom given up for adoption each year. Children's services informed us from the start that they would be reluctant to match us with a relinquished infant as there was always the risk that the birth parents would change their mind before the final court hearing and Daisy would lose her brother or sister after what could be months of bonding. This was something we were not prepared to put her or ourselves through. Tom was the relinquished baby we absolutely would never have. I suppose that's the first real lesson here. We were so busy opening our minds up to the daunting list of attributes we would, or could not, consider in our future child, that we almost dismissed the unexpected. Tom was in every possible sense of the word unexpected.

At the beginning of May 2008, Sarah, no younger than myself but on the receiving end of an infinitely different life experience, walked into her local hospital in labour. It was the first that any health professional or authority knew of her pregnancy and this, coupled with her insistence that she did not want to keep the baby, was the beginning of children's services' involvement. Already a mother of one, we know a little of the events that led up to her decision to give away her second born.

The information we have about Tom's birth family comes from Sarah and her mother, Tom's maternal grandmother. Sarah never took him home from hospital and it was six months later, after Tom's social worker, Jo, bound by procedure and protocol, had worked tirelessly to find him the right family as quickly as was possible, that we brought him home. The six months after birth are filled by courtesy of his foster carer.

Tom's background information is gathered in some semblance of order and can be found underneath our bed, accessible but not threatening – something that can be brought out and dipped into in manageable doses as Tom grows and matures enough to take ownership of what is rightfully his. A garish yellow, green and white cardboard box, with a matching lid upon which is attached a piece of A4 paper with the words Tom's Life History Box and a black and white computerised picture of an owl, it accompanied Jo, unannounced, one visit. What a box. All the known pieces of his jigsaw live inside. It is one of the most precious belongings we have in our home.

We have photographs of the many people who surrounded Tom's birth mother as she grew up and yet Tom was a concealed pregnancy with very few people except Sarah and her own mother knowing of his existence pre-birth. It is a testament to, or perhaps explanation for, Tom's stubborn, strong ways that he was as healthy as he was at birth. Happy as a child, Sarah is the youngest from a second marriage. Her beloved father died tragically in an accident. Sadly, we know Sarah suffered with serious depression. There is a story there to be pieced together one day by Tom and made sense of if possible. To help him with this unenviable task, children's services asked Sarah for as much information as they could, including the name of his birth father, but to this day she maintains she does not know it. Tom's birth father was a brief acquaintance of one night who, in all probability, is unaware that he fathered a noisy, truly quite beautiful son.

We are led to understand that Tom's maternal birth grandmother was upset about her daughter's decision to have Tom adopted, but did fully respect her daughter's wishes. It has been suggested to us by children's services that it was possibly too late to terminate the pregnancy when it was discovered, though Sarah's mother has stated, in a letter to Tom, that Sarah chose not to pursue this option. We'll not know the truth of the matter unless Tom has that frighteningly frank conversation with her one day in the future. All we can say is that she went through the ordeal of delivering the baby she had no intention or inclination to keep, insisting that she wanted the best for him. We will never be able to tell Tom what life was actually like for his birth mother, but we will be able to focus on the fact that she was resolute about what she wanted for him.

Sarah did not hold her baby after his birth but was later encouraged to do so, on arrival of the foster carer, which we understand she did reluctantly due to her determination to remain emotionally strong. Tom was named Billy by nurses who, I am sure, cared beautifully for him in those pivotal first hours in this big wide world. I struggle to think of him in that hospital without a mum, dad or a family. Alone. We were all out there. "Mum", "Dad" and "Day-day" (Daisy), grandparents, aunties and uncles too. We could have crowded round his hospital cot, got in the way of nurses, brought too many helium balloons, teddies and going home outfits. I've often wondered what it was I was doing that day; the day my son was born. I'd like to say I knew. I don't. I do know, however, what I was doing in the week of his birth, for I found out quite by accident very recently on a routine trip to see the nurse at our local doctors' surgery. I had my hormonal coil fitted. The week Tom was born and given up by his birth mother, I gave up the tiny chance, hope even, of conceiving our own child and resolved to move on, believing that our child was indeed out there already, waiting for us. I laughed nervously when the nurse said the date out loud, the anniversary of my coil fitting, though I felt like crying, felt sick and ecstatic all at once. Agreeing to come back in a year I said nothing more but fled home to see Tom. If only I could have held him the day he was born and told him I'd always be there for him.

In reality I wasn't even eligible at that stage. Sarah was

asked, encouraged, to have her photograph taken with her newborn baby for his future sake, and it was suggested she name him or accept the name the nurses had bestowed on him. And so Tom became known as Tom. A precious gift from his birth mother, and a birth family legacy, it was the preferred name, though not actual name, of her much loved maternal grandfather. The photo we have of Sarah holding Tom tells perfectly the story of a troubled young woman detached emotionally from the baby in her arms. She had let him go long before she said her tearful goodbye. I'll always feel an ache for her and what I perceive to be her pain. I feel a bond with someone I do not know at all. I can only hope that Tom will too. It would be fair to say that thanks to Sarah, her mother and a caring, competent children's service, we perhaps know more about our adopted child's birth mother and background than some adopters, or certainly as much, but we know only what she told them. Her active part in Tom's life was over before it even began.

Enter Cheryl the foster carer who, to all intents and purposes due to Tom's infancy, became his surrogate mother. During his first half-year Tom lived with an experienced foster family in a cold, damp cottage due for demolition. It says something about the shortage of foster carers and their position in the system as a valuable resource, when despite all this foster home's shortcomings it was highly prized by the local authority. Our introduction to him, our first week with him, was governed by someone who let her own feelings for Tom get in the way of doing her job. Nevertheless, he was undoubtedly loved by his single foster carer and especially by her five-year-old son. He was wanted.

While Tom was in foster care, children's services made extensive efforts to contact Sarah, trying to give her every opportunity within their power to change her mind and back down on her decision to have Tom adopted. But events spiralled for Sarah and she entered another tumultuous phase in her life when children's services temporarily removed her first born, Tom's half-brother, an apparently gorgeous well brought up boy, and placed him in the care of his birth father. Sarah's living accommodation had been deemed unsafe, not unclean, but a risk nonetheless to her child due to an inordinate amount of furniture that, it transpired, belonged to Sarah's mother. Sarah did exactly what she needed to do to get her first son back, and furthermore, she sought the medical help she was urged to have for her depression. Still she refused to change her mind about Tom, insisting that she was not ready for another baby and that there were things she needed to do for herself and her first born: a desire to return to study was key. We suspect the reality of giving away her own baby hit her as hard as anyone would imagine, and that for all her reluctance to acknowledge him, Sarah grieves for Tom in her own way.

As for Tom, he passed seemingly seamlessly, on the surface at least, from one person to the next and perhaps this does account for his absolute need for independence and wilful blinkered mindset. There are moments when we wonder whether certain dimensions of his personality can be attributed to the psychological impact that his first few days may have had on him. Being so young it is so hard to tell, but this is a path we are wary to tread. Not everything can be put down to what has gone before; some things are just typical baby, toddler, child, and teenage sort of things, just as my concerns, my worries, are typical mothering ones. It is possible, I believe, to think too much about adoption. In our house, our family, the person best at this is Daisy. Tom's being adopted never gets in the way of her understanding of him. She looks for nothing more than what he shows her and they understand each other. How we all came to be a family, that's really more for the grown-ups. Let the children get on with being just that: children.

Before tea time last night, and James home from work, we watched our two messing around under a bed sheet on the top landing of our three-storey town house. Squealing, laughing hysterically, they teetered dangerously close to the top of the stairs and then away again, ignoring pleas for calm and care, mucking around like siblings do: more powerful in their solidarity as a unit than their parents. Then naturally, and I say naturally with intended weight, came the obligatory falling out. Both in tears. On to the next thing they went: a very noisy, very wet bath time. A sister and a brother growing up together. But it didn't just happen. We were brought together. Form E and Form F did it – though Form E is now known by the more dignified name of Child's Permanence Report and Form F has become The Prospective Adopter's Report.

3

Daisy and Little One

Our biggest concern, the bottom line, was how exactly do two forms, two assessments, become a family? Was it really appropriate to apply a matchmaking process, more in depth but not entirely dissimilar to a blind date, to the future of our family? How did we prepare Daisy for adoption, when our own comprehension was still very much evolving and formulating as we went along? If we were flying by the seat of our pants, as I think we were in the beginning, how did we set about instilling understanding and maintaining a sense of normality and stability in our daughter? More to the point, what help did we need to do this? And what help did we get?

I don't mean to be flippant but the fact remains that most "normal" people look at us with a mixture of incredulity and utter disbelief, when they realise an adopter does not actually get to meet their future child until they have agreed the match. There are few who can suppress the look that flashes across their face, screeching, 'What? Are you mad?' before they manage to say, 'Really?' For most adopters this first meeting with their child can be a mere fourteen days, or even seven days like it was for us, before they take him or her home forever.

Putting aside the fact that you have not conceived this child who has had a life before you, it is possible to put this apparent raving lunacy into perspective. Comparisons can be drawn between adopted and biological children, as I remember saying to Daisy, while discussing her classmates' mixed understanding of Tom's legitimacy as her brother, of his official place in her life. 'I never met you, Daisy, until I met you.' She looked at me a little suspiciously, laughed but took it on the chin. 'Well, it's true.' I threw in a casual shrug for good measure, hoping to arm her with an easy quip that she could wheel out at school on demand. And it was true. What I omitted to tell her was that the scan I had late in my pregnancy with Daisy led us to believe she had the nose to rival Pinocchio, when actually anyone can see she has a perfectly proportioned button of a nose. I genuinely knew nothing more of her really; her gender, personality or looks, were all hidden in the rather grainy misleading profile. Though there was the insider knowledge that she brought out in me a rather naughty, probably unfounded, craving for doughnuts, fizzy, sour cola sweets and night after night of curry. The bond was a protective one and a promise of all that was to come: my dreams and hers.

As for adoption versus biological: Tom's status as a curious artefact from a foreign, unfamiliar process is fading for Daisy. She tends to get sidetracked nowadays with the whole birth thing. 'I came out of your bottom,' being her favourite intelligence of late. 'Sorry,' she corrects herself, 'Your front bottom.' Every so often I am treated to a rendition of all the different names her friends have for that particular part of a woman's anatomy: all of them rather fluffy terms but apparently fascinating nevertheless. Compared with that, adoption and all its social work jargon is quite frankly a bit boring. The physical possibility and yet seeming impossibility of birth prove far more intriguing.

Arguably, Daisy and her friends are a good age to accept

adoption. In the early school years they are encountering the concept of birth, of themselves being born; they are questioning differences in one another and the world around them. One of Daisy's friends, Kitty, thought that their disabled classmate had been born in his wheelchair. Now there's a thought. They live in a world in which it is common for families to be made up of brothers, half-brothers, stepbrothers, so once the initial fluster had settled, what was an adopted brother when thrown into the equation?

Children learn to understand the world around them as they learn their social behaviour and their ABC. They are born open minded. It's not such a bad thing, rather a good one in fact, that their learning curve encompasses as wide a sweep as possible, providing it is all age-appropriate knowledge. They tend to process it and move on, perhaps popping back now and again to make sure they have got it right.

For the adult, however, adoption requires the potential adopter to have faith in a rather plodding system: a system only as good as the people in it. At this stage of the process the most important person for us was still Daisy. Our future child was high in our priorities, but the reality is that you cannot possibly place the needs of an unknown child before, or even if we're honest, alongside, the needs of any existing children you may have. But for children's services, the interests of the children in their care are quite rightly paramount, and they will continually and understandably expect you to have the same perspective. Although this may not be natural or possible at this stage, ultimately the end goal is the same.

We chose to adopt through our local authority as they had been personally recommended to us and were touted as being superb at their jobs, if a little slow. It would be fair to say that this summary was by and large accurate. Due to no fault of their own they were admittedly slow at times but, due to the care and commitment of this team, our experience of adoption will always hold a very special place in our lives. We had faith in the system and the people in it never let us down. At the time that James and I made our initial enquiry we had wobbles; the adoption team had staffing problems due, we were informed, to illness and workload. It took over a year to get a place in the preparation groups and our assessment simply couldn't begin until then. For us, though it did not feel like it at times, this delay offered the perfect opportunity to ensure that we explored the possibility of life without a second child whilst allowing time to carefully consider the prospect of adoption. It was clear, however, that what we needed was answers to our questions. So by the time the groups did come round we were primed and ready to go. It took three years in total to have Tom, which for Daisy was half her lifetime.

Luckily for us, Daisy has always had a good concept of time and we were able to give her benchmarks to hold in her mind. Consequently, adoption was a factual event for her rather than the never-ending story it could so easily have seemed. To protect Daisy, and ourselves, we set about leading full lives and ensured that we did more than waiting for a brother or sister.

We felt that there was a fine line, a balance, between maintaining a sensible distance from adoption and being able to personalise what was, it could be said, an unnatural, very grown-up process for a child to undergo. The matching, for example: how to protect Daisy from the highs and lows, which would always come out of the blue and could turn her life upside down? We were keen to avoid the impact of this, and so Little One came to live with us, fleetingly at times, sometimes abandoned in the interests of here and now, at others very much at the heart of our daydreaming. Like an invisible childhood friend. By creating a sibling Daisy could identify with, we took

26

away some of the mystery. Little One was very much Daisy's younger brother or sister and Daisy was very much older, taller even, and had made room for him or her long before Tom's name was ever known to her. This we found not only helped, it also made for intriguing chit-chat at times when we ourselves perhaps were also feeling the wait.

Something we did have was time, and that's exactly what we took to filter in to Daisy's world a little more information on looked after children and the general process of adoption. We were not left to our own devices on this and our lovely social worker, Aggie, ensured that Daisy was never made to feel excluded. In fact it was Aggie, about two months into our assessment, who supplied Daisy with the best breakdown of the adoption process that we have come across; a print-out of *Bridget's taking a long time* was given to Daisy to colour in and read over at leisure. Aggie encouraged Daisy to change the names in it to match our own. The story clearly described the procedures we would be following within a family setting and featured a little girl who was impatient to meet her new brother or sister. It was a benefit to us all. James referred back to this publication on several occasions simply to clarify in his mind exactly what was happening and what would, should, be happening next, which thoroughly amused Daisy and made her feel just that little bit more involved.

Other than this, there was very little out there to read aimed specifically at existing children in a family about to adopt. Since then, BAAF has produced a booklet written for birth children called *Adopting a brother or sister*; too late to prepare Daisy, but she has read it with interest and given it her seal of approval!

Daisy took matters into her own hands and got stuck right in. On the day of our first interview with Aggie, I got a call from Daisy's school. She came home feeling "unwell" halfway through the morning, comfortably in time for Aggie's arrival. Making a miraculous recovery, she quickly set about spelling out SCHOOL SUCKS on the fridge in magnet alphabet letters for all to see, before moving on to rhyme Aggie's name with every possible unsuitable word: saggy, baggy, haggy, daggy, and more. She then sat throughout the session, supposedly drawing, but instead drafting and completing adoption forms of her own, and copying Aggie's movements as she did so. Suffice it to say Aggie and Daisy hit it off from the start and to this day Daisy has a very positive view of Aggie and consequently of children's services. She maintained for some time after that she wanted to be a social worker when she grows up.

Further to their impromptu meeting of minds at our first assessment session, and just a few weeks later, Daisy had her very own session with Aggie, which for me proved to be one of the more painful parts of the process. To watch my little girl sit so diligently and seriously, desperate to help, ready to stand up and be counted in this family effort, really touched me. Aggie could not have been any lovelier, and as Daisy unquestioningly underwent an adoption assessment, drawing sad faces, angry faces, and happy faces on demand, I felt upset that it had come to this, and perhaps proud that she was the child she was. I could see how hard she was trying; I didn't even get the eye contact to give her one of my winks, so attentively did she approach the task. The answers to Aggie's questions: 'When have you seen an angry face, Daisy?' came very honestly, very easily. 'Daddy – Daddy sometimes looks angry.' There she was, my baby, helping us have another child. We truly were a team and I was so sorry that I had been unable to take care of it all like other mums do. Daisy seemed unperturbed.

It fell to Einstein to lighten the moment. Our back door needed to be clicked firmly into place in order to be deemed "shut" and in the excitement of Aggie's arrival this hadn't happened. Despite being ousted into the garden, Einstein decided that as he had a visitor, it would be rude not to give her his customary greeting. Jumping up at the back door, he pushed it open and, fresh from a good old mooch and rummage in our wet and wintry garden, launched himself at Aggie, who was sitting with Daisy at our dining room table in the middle of a deep and meaningful conversation. Attempting to clamber onto her previously clean and neat lap (he continues to have delusions that he is a lap dog), Einstein enthusiastically embarked on licking her face free of make-up. Aggie made a polite comment about his strength and suggested we work a little on the impression that he might make on our new child and referred briefly back to the "Big Dog" form, as we called it, that we had filled out earlier in our assessment. The threat that big dogs can pose to some children means they, like their owners, must also be assessed. Daisy and I looked at each other, suppressing the twitch at the corner of our mouths, and I, in an attempt to move on, nodded earnestly in agreement.

Aggie was perfectly happy. She felt that Daisy was very switched on and realistic about what she could expect. Nevertheless, Aggie gently but persistently made sure to push home the point that there would be arguments, sharing, and what's more, a birth family in the background. Then, to finish the session, she rather cleverly got Daisy to take her round our house. It was the first time that Aggie had seen further than downstairs, and it was a good method to encourage Daisy to chat more informally and perhaps to feel even more involved. And that was the end of Daisy's one-to-one session to prepare her for adoption.

It was interesting that my "Black Sunday", my day of panic and doubt, immediately followed. In my eyes we were one phone call away from putting it all behind us. I boldly put this to Daisy, wondering, waiting to see if she would be relieved. She cried and begged us to go ahead, which was all we needed to hear.

As for Einstein, how we were ever going to get him through the assessment with all his well-intentioned high spirits, we didn't know. But he was as much a part of our family and Daisy's world as we were, and we had promised ourselves that we would offer the adoption team the real us. If that wasn't right for an infant, then an infant wasn't right for us, and so we happily, laughingly, quite earnestly expected to adopt a robust, not so little, pre-school-age child or older. One who could withstand the "wag factor" at least.

Little One popped in only now and again in the early days, but became a regular visitor and topic of conversation as we followed further along the adoption trail. The transformation, just before the start of the home visits, of our tiny third bedroom into a gorgeous, homely little cocoon was a landmark moment for Daisy – 'I love it. Can I sleep in it?' 'That's Little One's room,' she would casually, purposefully, inform friends who came to play. On the day that we assembled the cot bed she arrived in the room with armfuls of her own toys, full of love and caught up in the moment. For her, Little One had just taken a step closer and she was beginning to feel something very real for an imaginary brother or sister.

The weekend before our Monday panel, which would, or would not, recommend us as adopters, we happily attended two birthday parties on the Saturday, followed by a christening on the Sunday. The well wishing and moral boosting efforts began in earnest. We had the full support of everyone around us but more importantly we were busy. However, we could delay the anticipation no longer. At half past five on the Monday morning I heard Daisy, awake and unsettled, taking books out from her bookshelf and putting them back again. Somehow we got through the morning routine and walked Daisy to school. She was fully aware of the importance of the day, in line with our open, age-appropriate policy. We felt confident enough about the outcome by this stage, and Daisy needed to see some progress. More importantly, she understood that we would be fine with or without another child. We had done everything we could to get to this point. We knew she would be kept busy at school so that the importance of the day would diffuse, and we alerted her teacher to what was going on. Daisy quickly ran through our routine again with me. If it was a "yes" we would be waiting in the playground at "home time" with a helium balloon so that she would be able to see at a glance rather than having to queue up, wait for the teacher to spot us and do the long walk over before knowing.

Subsequently the very big, very pink helium balloon bobbed around in the air and James and I, emotional, exhausted but exuberantly triumphant stood waiting to scoop Daisy up and celebrate. Through the window we saw the children line up in the classroom with their teacher, ready to come home, and at that moment, for the first time since all this began, I knew that Daisy herself knew she was definitely going to be a big sister one day.

Only she didn't. As it happened, she had desperately scanned for a balloon, which she had spotted easily enough, but had been unable to see who was holding it, and Daisy being Daisy, hadn't dared take for granted that it was us and that it was meant for her. It was as she coyly ambled out, her schoolbook bag and her coat trailing behind her, and saw us – it was only then that Daisy knew for sure she was going to be a big sister. Little One was closer than ever. She didn't say much. What she did say neither one of us can recall. That night we three went out for a celebratory tea, though really we were all too tired to enjoy the moment. It was a day for jubilation but that could wait. We drank champagne. We toasted 'us'. We flopped.

Daisy didn't know that Aggie had that very day told us about a little boy she thought could have been suitable but for whom we were being approved too late. Was this pointless, painful news? I think not. We had opted to be informed, and though difficult, this was the reality and something we were going to have to protect Daisy from. We spared Daisy any detail about the panel other than the resounding "yes", but made sure to tell her that the Chair had complimented us on having such a lovely, well grounded daughter, and that Einstein had not even been deemed worthy of a mention, though we all agreed it was best not to tell him that.

Daisy broke up from school for the summer at the end of that week and shortly after that we were made aware of a three-year-old girl, with red hair, who was not yet fully ready for matching due to a medical query, but for whom our names had been put forward for consideration. Our hearts surged a little and for one moment we allowed ourselves to think "What if?" We were never to hear any more. She wasn't Little One. It made us grateful that Daisy knew nothing, for how many more would there be? We were going to have to be very careful. Daisy, it was agreed by all, was not to know about any possible match until it was confirmed.

In late August we set off to the South of France to a fairytale tower with shutters set amongst stunning pine and rosemary woodland on the Cote D'Azure in Provence. It was a gift to ourselves, to the three of us for getting this far, and here, in the magical setting, we swam in the sea, made sandcastles, went on adventures in the hillside woodland, brushed up our French, got laughed at, visited nearby towns and terrified ourselves on the winding, cliff hugging roads that lead to charming Saint Tropez. It wasn't until the last night that I said to James: 'I'm ready now. I want to go home. Little One's out there and I want to get back and get on with things.'

Back home, that's exactly what we did. Daisy started her final year at the infant school, I had my very long hair cut to above my chin, put our names down for three rescue battery hens and started my own vintage dress business online. Aggie rang to check in with us and her message was clear. 'There's nothing for you. Get on with the rest of your lives.'

'Absolutely,' I agreed. I took the call outside whilst clearing a spot for the chicken coop: something I omitted to tell Aggie in case there were more forms to fill in and we would then only be matched with a big-sister, ridiculous-dog, three-cat, chicken-friendly-child. We could be in for a wait and a half. 'That's OK,' I told Daisy, 'We're good at that.'

It was only two weeks later, Tuesday 30 September 2008, in the car on the way to the supermarket, Daisy safely tucked away at school, that I laughingly said to James, 'After all this we'll end up being matched with a baby. I've just got a funny feeling Little One is a baby boy.' Where this conviction came from I'm not sure, but we both know exactly where we were when I said it, so poignant in hindsight as it is. Once home, we struggled in the door with the week's food haul, fending off Einstein who was torn between more food than he could shake a leg at and love of us, and without thought I routinely checked for messages on our home phone. One. It was Aggie and by the little she said, the tone of her voice, I knew instantly without doubt what this moment was. Everything else slipped out of focus and I went hot and cold all at once and literally trembled as I relayed the message to James. We both agreed that he should call her back, being far less emotional than I. The food shop could wait. I pottered uselessly trying to behave myself, to not interrupt and gesticulate wildly as I am prone to do when James is on the phone, and I came to rest on the toy box in the dining room where James was at the table scribbling down notes. There was a baby. A four-month-old-boy. We were not to get excited. I thought of Daisy unknowing at school. Ignoring Aggie's experienced and sound advice, it was at this precise moment that I fell in love with Tom. Once off the phone James repeated all the information and I sat there on the pale blue wooden toy box that now contains some of his many toys, and sobbed.

We were to wait until Monday 6 October to see if we had been chosen by Tom's social worker. She had our Form F and would be looking at it over the weekend. There was no way we were letting this slip by us and so Top Secret Operation Tom began. For two weeks, friends and family helped us desensitise Einstein to visitors. Our aim was to curb his enthusiasm, for although we knew how lovely and gentle he was, we wanted Tom's social workers to give us a chance, and felt that having a 30 kilo Labrador on top of you joyfully licking your face wasn't the winning impression we should be aiming for. We gathered photographs to show him in his true much gentler, soppier colours and Daisy, without understanding the urgency, threw herself into training her four-legged best friend in the belief that Aggie might pop in to see how he was doing and that it might help us find Little One that little bit sooner. Everyone was on board, everyone knew something was up but no one knew the full story and no one was allowed to let anything slip to Daisy.

On Monday 13 October Aggie arrived early, almost as nervous as we were. We hit it off with Jo and Jane, Tom's social workers, straight away. How we managed to get three such wonderful, positive and likeable social workers we still don't know. We were eager for information about Tom. Would we get past the Einstein factor? As luck would have it, Jane had grown up with Labradors, Tom's foster carer's parents had a Labrador and, most importantly, both Jo and Jane had a fabulous sense of humour. As for Einstein, he was close to angelic, something I never thought I would say, and we discovered during the visit that they were not considering anyone else for Tom. As they told us about the little boy who would become our son, about how he had been concealed, given up at birth, about his development and the vulnerability of his birth mother, I fell deeper and deeper in love. Without it ever being said, James and I felt they thought us to be the match for Tom. They offered to show us the photographs of Tom and it was only then that I realised it hadn't mattered to us what he looked like – we just simply wanted him. This was our son. I knew it was meant to be. And then it was time for them to leave, taking the photos with them.

Both James and I were on a high. It felt good. It felt right. We would be knocked for six if we were not now chosen. Once again I was glad Daisy knew nothing of this. Jo and Jane promised they would call us very soon, though it wouldn't be the same day. We collected ourselves together, and then Daisy from school, glancing at each other joyously; full of the secret we couldn't tell as we watched her skip home in front of us. We think you've got a baby brother.

The next day James was back at work. I walked Daisy to school and then popped in to my parents' house – they were away on holiday – to sort post and water plants. I clutched my mobile phone the whole time, praying for the call that would change all our lives forever, preparing myself that maybe they had had second thoughts. Back home I was in the toilet and it was then, of course, that the phone rang. Sparing no blushes I ran, trousers round my knees, into the lounge and answered it, taking a deep breath as I did. It was Jo. They loved us. They thought we'd be perfect. 'I'm ringing with really good news,' she said in a grave voice that could give me reason to think otherwise. I shook, not for the first time of late. She said how impressed she had been with our positive attitude to Tom's birth mother. I promised her then and there that we would love that little boy, give him everything and more that he deserved, and she said, 'I know you will, I know you will.'

Off the phone I squealed and bounced up and down clutching at my trousers in front of a bemused Einstein. I wanted to stand in a field and scream. Somehow I ended up outside the back door with no shoes on when really I wanted to be outside the front door with shoes on and car keys in hand. This was news to be told in person. I drove as if on my driving test, repeatedly reminding myself to stop at junctions, go round roundabouts to the left, and can still remember admiring the gorgeous autumn colours of the trees on Birches Lane. I even managed to fill the car up with petrol before abandoning it outside James' shop and flinging myself at him in a big bear hug: 'We've done it!'

Sort of, anyway. Daisy still wasn't to know a thing. Tom was not as yet free for adoption. Sarah, his birth mother, could still change her mind though she had agreed that we could have her medical record, which was, we were told, a good sign as it meant she wasn't wavering. She had also said that she didn't want to meet us – another good sign, Aggie said, as it suggested she had no intention of attaching to Tom. Sad but nonetheless true. I was disappointed not to meet her, for Tom's future sake, and I was curious too, but realised it was a lot to ask for and understood how intimidating it would be if I were in her situation. James was relieved.

There would be two further weeks of waiting. During these Daisy named a cuddly toy panda of hers "Tommy" and started saying things like, 'I've decided I really want a baby brother, Mummy.' We checked ourselves again and again, grilled friends and family hoping to find the weakest link, the leak, for by now a few nearest and dearest knew we were the "chosen ones". We asked Daisy as leading questions as we dared, but to this day she maintains she hadn't got a clue. Everyone behind the scenes was proceeding as if it were to happen: Aggie cautious, Jo positive and determined, and us with blind faith. We were warned of possible court delays, something we hoped desperately would not happen. There were both tears and laughter during those two weeks and all without letting on to Daisy.

The day of the court hearing to free Tom for adoption

arrived. Friday 14 November 2008. "Children in Need" day. Ironically it was also National Adoption Week. Daisy and I were determined: she to wear her "Children in Need" mascot: "Pudsey Bear Ears" all day at school, and me to end Tom's rather cloak and dagger start to life. Let there be no delay, let this end now. I walked Daisy to school, walked home and vacuumed for England like a pregnant woman nesting at full term and on the basis that it was unlikely they would ring early. It was whilst vacuuming that I found the note and gift from James who knew I'd be under the beds sucking up every last pet hair, and so under Tom's future cot is where he put them. I still have the note: 'Take ten minutes and relax with these and a cuppa with Pudsey Bear. See you later Mummy xx.' So doing as I was told for once, I stopped to eat chocolate and drink tea from my "Children in Need" mug whilst checking my emails. At 10am the phone rang. It was Jo. The case had whipped through the court. Tom was free for adoption. I simply couldn't believe it. After phoning James I made a call or two to those closest to us, reminding them that Daisy did not yet know a thing about any of this. When I picked her up from school I confided in close friend Chloe, Holly's mum, but spent as little time as possible in the playground to avoid the eyes of other friendly, inquisitive people who knew nothing other than that something was up. As I stood and watched Daisy run towards me, her pink duffle coat flapping, I truly felt I would burst with happiness. When we arrived home there was a huge bouquet of blue and white flowers on the doorstep with the message, 'The best things come to those who wait, All our love James, Daisy and Tom.' I quickly hid the card from Daisy and laughed it off as 'Silly Daddy'. She thought it terribly romantic. 'Daddy loves you,' she said.

Daisy and I read together, played a board game and I ran her a bath filled with butterfly bath confetti and enjoyed the last few moments of it just being us in her little head. Just us girls together. I let slip that we had something we wanted to talk to her about as I didn't want the news to come completely out of the blue. Her senses were immediately heightened.

I have a photo of Daisy, innocent and unknowing, taken shortly before James came home that evening. In it she looks so happy and it reminds me every time I see it just how important it is that whatever James and I choose to do must never be allowed to change that happiness. When James did arrive home we sat her on the sofa between us and I clutched an A4 envelope. 'What do you think might be in this?' I asked, 'Daddy and I really want to talk to you about something.'

'Have I done something wrong? Is it my school photograph?' she asked earnestly.

'No, but it is a photograph, well, a small photocopy of a photograph,' I answered, barely able to contain myself. The proper photos were due to arrive after the weekend, after the panel had approved our match on Monday, a formality we were supposed to wait for before revealing all to Daisy. 'Inside is a photo of your baby brother. His name is Tom and he's only six months old.' I waited as the news sank in and she searched my face for signs of truth. Clutching the piece of paper, eyes sparkling, pint-sized Daisy grew just a few more inches. 'He's so cute. He's gorgeous.' Over the next few hours Daisy rang her grandparents, aunties and uncles and her best friend Holly to share her important news.

'I've got a baby brother and his name is Tom.'

I realise now that it was one of the best times in our lives, certainly the most momentous, although we were too caught up at the time and embroiled in the huge effort it had taken to fully appreciate how happy a time it was. Daisy was delighted. 14 November 2008 was special, and yet we can remember little apart from Daisy sitting on the sofa, holding the little grainy square photocopy of her baby brother. We all waited for the weekend to pass and for the panel to approve us. It was functional. We needed to get it out of the way. We played this one down with Daisy, confident that they would approve, crazy maybe, risky perhaps, but we were on top of the world and nothing was going to stop us now.

I walked into Tom's room on the Monday morning, "matching panel day", and winding up his blind as I had done every morning since decorating, I found myself addressing the room, filling him in, I guess, on what was happening. The phone call came just after 11am while Daisy and James were at school and work respectively. It was Aggie. Jo was with her. I spoke to them both. We were done. We were on. James, Daisy, Tom and I were to be a family.

A good job, for in our hearts we were already there. It had long since stopped being about forms and formality. Adoption for us was now very real with some very real people at the heart of it. Looking back, I can honestly say that Daisy had been protected from most of the anxieties of adoption. She was a little wiser than her friends on the matter, more aware of the concept, well informed about the bare bones of the process. Children's services did a great job and it was clear that Aggie, alongside the happiness and welfare of our future child, did have Daisy at the forefront of her thoughts.

It was at the next stage that Daisy was let down. Not by one individual but by a system and, as is often the case in life, a set of circumstances. There was no lasting damage and the ending promises to be the happy one every child's story should have but Daisy was exposed to more than we feel was appropriate, and it left her exhausted both emotionally and physically. Matters can get rather complicated when they involve the heart. We are all only human after all.

4

The baby thieves

The introductions were set to commence on Monday 24 November 2008. It was a day on which Daisy was to go to school as normal and we were to attend a planning meeting with children's services and Tom's foster carer, Cheryl, whom we had neither met nor spoken to before. We were told that it was after this meeting that we were quite possibly, not definitely, but certainly hopefully to meet our son for the first time. What a carrot to dangle. That was, of course, if it didn't all have to be rearranged due to the heavy snowfall throughout the county. Sledges at the ready, we moved forward, as always purposefully, for there had been too many unknowns for too long. These introductions were happening by hook or, a festive Shepherd's, crook.

The wait for them to begin, albeit only a couple of weeks from the point of telling Daisy about her new status as big sister, was perhaps, for her especially, the longest yet. It was also, however, the most fun. We were buoyant and able, for the first time ever, to talk freely about our son, Daisy's brother, and what's more we could now legitimately buy items for him to help welcome him into his new life. There was no doubt that this was a good time and one we had long since earned the right to enjoy.

But our highs were rarely without lows. Most notably so when, on Friday 21 November 2008, three days before our introductions were due to start, a genuinely lovely lady who showed continued interest and support throughout, asked for her regular update and I rather excitedly brought her up to speed with the latest developments. 'Lovely,' she said before continuing, 'of course my friend adopted and her two children couldn't handle it.' The punch line came too quickly for me to intervene or for her to think it through, 'they ended up committing suicide.' Daisy had been there by my side the whole time. Sometimes I wonder whether a more secretive approach to adoption would have ultimately spared Daisy a few unnecessary experiences.

Talking only last weekend to a friend of ours, who has herself recently adopted, she pointed out how graciously she thought Daisy had handled herself throughout. She's right, and never more so than during the introductions. Daisy went off on Monday 24 November to do a full day at school without a quibble, knowing full well that James and I might, or might not, be meeting her baby brother that day; without her. Furthermore, it was as yet still unconfirmed exactly when it would be her turn, her opportunity. This must have been both daunting and frustrating but she accepted it graciously and went about her business with dignity.

I write this chapter a year to the month after we lived through these events and so it was very gently yesterday that I touched on our introductions to Tom with Daisy, and the first thing she said was, 'Do you remember how I cried when we had to leave Tom there on the last night, Mummy?' Oh I do. I will never forget.

It began as it ended. Cheryl was crying as we entered the meeting room, which though in the same county, felt far away from anywhere near home. Turned down herself on her written request to adopt Tom, it was understandable that parting with him was going to be painful for his young foster carer and I felt terrible that she had to go through it. There has to be a lot that is good in a person who falls in love with a child not officially regarded as their own, and who wishes to care for him forever. Moreover, Cheryl had been through the intensely difficult experience, and honour some might say, of taking Tom home from hospital just two days after his birth.

There were six faces from children's services present at the planning meeting, only three of which were familiar. In an effort to start as we meant to go on, I plumped for the seat next to Cheryl, anxious that we do this together to avoid the strained relations with foster carers that we had heard about from past adopters. During the planning meeting the Chair was very sensitive: she attempted to make it clear to James and me that Cheryl's crying should not make us feel unable to assert ourselves. Sadly it did. It set the tone the week was to take. I hoped desperately that Cheryl would resign herself to the inevitable: it was, sadly for her, a done deal; a decision that we had absolutely nothing to do with.

It was obvious that Cheryl had not been prepared by her support system for this separation, at least not sufficiently, and though we exchanged a couple of niceties and I fed her a constant supply of tissues (glad I hadn't grabbed the usual handful of toilet roll), things were not off to the positive start we had hoped for and had naively expected at this stage of the process.

It was a terrible feeling to sit there, the cause of all those tears, and if it hadn't been for the fact that everyone there knew how carefully we had been chosen, I could have readily burst into floods of tears myself and apologised profusely for even dreaming to take her baby and left there and then.

Although the introductions were everything that we had wanted and worked for, they were also the worst part of our adoption experience to date and I am sorry that I was not strong enough to say, 'Enough is enough, this is not acceptable'. The thing is, we were so damn grateful to even be there that we nodded away enthusiastically and agreed to whatever everyone else felt was best. How hard could one week be, and weren't we getting Tom out of it? But Tom was to be subjected to a lot of driving backwards and forwards – on some days most of our time with him would be spent in the car – and as for Daisy, she came way down the list of priorities. A list that appeared to have, in order: Cheryl; Sam, the foster carer's five-year-old son; Tom himself; then James and me; followed by children's services; with Daisy well at the bottom. We were led and we followed, trying our best not to rock the boat or upset anybody as we went. In doing so we let down our daughter. 'But it wasn't your fault, Mum.' It was though. It was my job, my responsibility together with James to get it right, and we almost lost the plot at the last stage.

As well as the crying, we did manage to cover the ins and outs of Tom's milk requirements, bedtime routine, likes and dislikes, weight and other notables. At the end of the meeting I handed Cheryl a wonderful book we had bought that enables a new adoptive family, or any family for that matter, to record sound bite messages and introductions to family members with photographs. It had been lovingly prepared at home. As I handed it to her, in order for her to read though it that week with Tom to support our visits, I thought about the effort that Daisy had put into it and the fits of giggles we had trying to record the messages and sound effects. The photo of Daisy and her message still brings a lump to my throat now: 'I'm your big sister Daisy,' her voice as proud as could be. The photograph itself was taken on the day, only an hour or so before, we told Daisy about Tom. It was the happy photo I have mentioned previously, our benchmark for how Daisy had truly fared since our decision to adopt. What I handed to Cheryl in that room was not just a gesture, an aid for Tom to adjust to our ugly mugs and familiarise himself with our voices, it was all Daisy's hopes and dreams. I trusted Cheryl, an adult, to handle that with due care and consideration.

After the meeting on that first day, James and I retired to a recommended well-known garden centre situated close to children's services for a miserable lunch and attempted to pull ourselves together. I nipped into the toilets and, despite our being out of area, happened to bump into a familiar face from school. The poor woman got a shambolic, rather nervous, rambling answer to her unsuspecting, 'What are you doing here?' before I left her wishing us well and rushed back to our table to re-read the comforting text message from my mum. We were less than an hour away from meeting Tom. I'm not sure I could quite believe it. Was I really to have another baby after all? I remember thinking that I must be the luckiest woman alive and that I must not allow myself to forget that over the course of the week. This was the biggest mistake of all.

On finding Cheryl's house we looked at one another in that 'Let's do it' kind of way. We were on our own now. No social workers, just someone who didn't want us there, our new son who had never ever seen us before and us two beginners.

It was an unforgettably cold house, an old cottage, rightly due for demolition. Cheryl answered the door and let us in. As we stepped inside her lounge this beautiful baby, lying on his tummy, turned his head and gave us this huge, silly gummy grin. And there it was, the moment we first met Tom.

Tom was the easy bit. For me it was like being handed my newborn baby and now we were going to start to get to know one another. Not so. For one week, seven long days, thankfully not more due to his very young age, we listened to repeated loops of how much Cheryl and her extended family doted on him. Unbeknown to children's services, this extended family seemed to pop up and in at every opportunity; we were politely interviewed and vetted by them all.

To be crystal clear, I understood their love, and will appreciate it for the rest of my life, and am grateful to them; I know that no amount of vetting would be enough for me to leave my two children with strangers. Yet we had already jumped through every possible hoop for children's services, we had been assessed and approved, and now deserved the chance to just get on and be ourselves so that Cheryl could see why three social workers had chosen us for Tom. Moreover, we would have preferred a chance to bond with the adorable baby boy we watched being passed around amongst Cheryl's family. It wasn't to be. We were so close and yet still so very far away from all that we had dreamt of. Our introduction to Tom was treated as their goodbye – something we feel the extended family should most certainly have done prior to our arrival.

To make matters more intense, at around four o'clock on the first day, Cheryl's son, Sam, came home from school while back home our family picked up Daisy from her school and looked after her for us. Sam proceeded, quite rightly, to check us out, but mainly he stuck to Tom like glue. It was clear from the end of the first day that we were taking his baby brother. The system had let Sam down. No one, it seemed, had prepared him for his loss even though it was an expected and imminent one. Grief was to dominate the entire week and not our bonding with Tom or the formation of attachment.

Reluctantly, considering the raw feelings so obviously seething underneath the cool politeness inside Cheryl's home, it was time for Daisy to be introduced into the picture. On the Tuesday, James, Daisy and I got up at the crack of dawn and bundled Daisy off to her grandparents who were to take her to school, to enable James and me to be there when Tom woke up. That day, as was typical of every day spent in Cheryl's company, we did manage to communicate at times and, after having spent much of the day sitting on the floor, we even helped her with the delivery of her new sofas. We wanted nothing more than to get on with her and Sam. However, the very reason for our being there continued to be the sticking point.

We had told Daisy that first night of the introductions that she was going to get picked up from school halfway through the next day, and spend the late afternoon with Tom right until his bedtime at Cheryl's. What actually happened was that Daisy sat and watched as Sam territorially guarded what Daisy had been led to believe by everyone else was her new baby brother.

We had warned Daisy how hard this was for Cheryl and Sam but we needn't have bothered. They did that themselves and made sure that our little girl knew exactly what she was doing to them. James and I had to gently but firmly step in before Daisy got at least some snatched time with Tom away from Sam. Once Sam had been tearfully extracted by Cheryl from the bathroom, the three of us bathed Tom on our own that second night. There, in that bathroom, we took precious photographs of the four of us alone for the first time: hiding out. They remind me of photographs taken immediately after the birth of a child: wide eyes, shattered people smiling because they know they will be very happy, should be very happy, just perhaps a little too numb right then to feel it. Tom took to us beautifully and, apart from the cold, we actually had a few moments of fun. Daisy didn't like leaving him at the end of her first visit and it was a very subdued Daisy we took home.

She didn't like several things. 'The way it feels being at Cheryl's,' and 'He doesn't have anything,' she mused, and it was true that Tom had very few personal belongings to call his own. And she was troubled by his standard of living: 'Why is he not in a real cot?' 'Why did he turn purple in the bathroom?'

Other than clothes, Tom had very little and had spent his life so far sleeping in a travel cot. He was quite obviously feeling the cold and damp for his nose was permanently red, he had a purple tinge to his arms and hands that came and went, and a persistent chesty cough. Due to circulation problems Tom is particularly susceptible to the cold though now, thankfully, only suffers when exposed to the elements outside. We were well aware, and attempted to reason with Daisy, that single mother Cheryl had created a secure, loving home without the luxuries we had, and perhaps even with few essentials, but one where Tom was at least wanted. 'Well, I wish we could bring him home now,' she said. Me too, but there was a plan to follow, and at this early stage we would never have dreamed of deviating from it.

The plan for the week worked one way, and that was Cheryl's way, and we followed it to the letter in the beginning except, it seemed, when Cheryl wanted to change it without notice. The third day, as planned, Daisy was off school to enable her to travel over late morning with us to Cheryl's and for her to give Tom his lunch. This was something she had proudly made sure to tell the grandparents. But when we arrived Cheryl announced, rather too casually, that she had fed Tom his lunch at her mother's that morning. We were dumbfounded but at such an early stage of the introductions, stranded at her house, we were reluctant to confront her. Daisy was gutted but said nothing, only looked at me, her head held high, disappointment stinging her eyes but too polite to let it fall down her cheeks. What did I do about it? Well, I questioned it coldly and referred briefly to the planning meeting Cheryl so frequently referred to herself but I did nothing more. Spleens could be vented later.

It was a peculiar feeling, a little out on a limb, to be

there in Cheryl's home. At the end of the day, Cheryl was allowing us in and putting up with us in her home, and bearing in mind the reason for our being there, this must have been a tremendous strain on her. Perhaps that is why Cheryl received several phone calls from children's services and family members asking her, in front of us, how it was going. It would be fair to say she was hardly generous in her answers, 'It's OK, yeah they seem OK. It's hard to tell,' was one of the more memorable feedback snippets she gave. Cheryl had a visit from her social worker whilst we were there and then another from Tom's life story book worker.

Meanwhile, we received two evening phone calls of our own back at our home, one mid-week and the other at the end of the week, and we were advised when voicing our concerns to more or less grin and bear it. Which, don't get me wrong, was to some extent right. It was only a week. We could hang on to what it was we were there to get out of it. Tom was worth anything and everything. How hard could it be? Trust me, if you ever do it, it can be very hard though it should not have to be.

This is where we began to wise up. I was not going to upset further someone who, whilst obviously intent on having things her way, was having a very hard time of it. It was quite clear that we were going to have to survive and find our own ways to ensure bonding time with Tom for his sake more than ours, for in less than six days' time he was to come and live with us forever – and what preparation was he getting for that?

On the Wednesday, the third day, when pushed to the limit by "how hard it was for her", I ended up firmly pointing out to Cheryl that we had actually had a particularly difficult time ourselves, for many years now, and that no matter how hard this was for her and her family, we absolutely needed and deserved this to go well and so did Tom. I stressed that perhaps Sam was not the only child to be finding this difficult. To her credit, Cheryl took Sam aside and had her firmest words yet with him. A mother myself, it was impossible not to feel terribly sorry for him: another innocent bystander on our adoption journey.

It was on this day that we were scheduled to go out with Tom alone for a couple of hours, without Cheryl and her entourage, and we were supposed to head somewhere local. The well-known garden centre whose miserable lunch we had endured was suggested. Turning round in the driver's seat of our car, having just helped James buckle our two children in, I saw them alone together for only the second time ever. I caught my breath. Then, in the way that every good mother should, I said, 'sod that'. Tom was a six-month-old baby. One garden centre would seem the same as any other. What could possibly be more upsetting and unsettling for him than the scenes unfolding and the tension building in Cheryl's house? 'Let's head for more familiar shores,' and so we hightailed it to a garden centre in the town next to ours, which was a more reassuring stomping ground for us, for Daisy, and here, in stolen time, we mooched among the Christmas displays, bought a decoration or two for our home and had cake and drinks whilst Tom sat grinning and giggling happily in a highchair, charming all who passed by.

In our own space at last, able to relax a little, it became apparent that Tom adored Daisy. He was transfixed by her and she could do no wrong. That relationship still reigns. I would go so far as to say that it was Daisy whom Tom loved first. He fell asleep in the car on the way back to Cheryl's holding on tightly to Daisy's hand. I call this part of Tom's adoption, 'bonding done our way'.

Refreshed enough to return, on time, we felt a little rebellious and more resilient to the onslaught of, 'Do you know how hard this is for us?' In fact, we felt more alive again. We had reminded ourselves what this was all supposed to be about. It was our way of clawing back some control, I think. Maybe it was a bit naughty but it was definitely the right sort of naughty.

To Daisy and Sam's credit they also managed to get on rather well and played together beautifully, though the atmosphere changed very quickly at random, and Daisy would often find herself caught, in a strange lady's house in the middle of goodness knows where, with a boy more or less the same age as her who made her feel like, we were taking Cheryl's baby away.

We refrained, and still have to this day, to mention our own bending of the introduction arrangements and, in fact, pride ourselves quietly on using our initiative to adjust the plan as we saw fit. It is to our credit and nobody else's, rightly or wrongly, that Tom had such a smooth transition into our lives, but to our shame that we were not stronger to begin with. Obviously, as a course of action for other potential adopters, we would recommend prevention rather than cure.

We went on to find other ways of making the introductions seem more of a positive event than they were when holed up at Cheryl's. We registered Tom with our doctor, which was a wonderfully practical, rather reassuring thing to do in such an unsettled week. An anchor for the future, maybe.

On the fourth day Daisy was left completely out of the arrangements and packed off, once again at dawn, to the grandparents in order for them to be able to take her to school whilst we arrived at Cheryl's before Tom woke up. And still Daisy made no fuss. Perhaps she was relieved to have a day off? James and I spent the first half of the day with Tom. Inspired by the quality of time that yesterday's escapade had given us, we sneaked him back to another town near home for a spot of Christmas shopping. We even popped home to introduce him to his very own bedroom complete with cot and quality mattress and more toys than were strictly necessary. We showed him the garden, and allowed the furry, four-legged members of our family to come and smell him and gently suss him out. He took to them immediately, in particular the cats who very kindly went on to allow him to come and live with us; in return his very first word was to be 'at'. This was a most precious time for us and it helped us regain some sanity and balance. We returned him promptly after lunch as agreed and once more refrained from letting Cheryl know.

Finally the next day, with Daisy involved from beginning to end, and five days into a seven-day plan, Tom was to "officially" visit his new home with Cheryl accompanying him. Sam, who by now was biting and kicking as well as crying during our visits, was not to be included. After making her feel welcome, and I have to say this was easy and important for us to do as we were determined to turn the introductions into a more uplifting experience for all concerned, Cheryl was to leave us to it until mid-afternoon. It was a successful day and the first sign that she had indeed switched into a more professional mode.

That evening, just the three of us again, we threw ourselves into the town's "Christmas Light Switch On" celebrations. Daisy revelled in the late night shopping opportunity to buy Tom gifts and deliberated quite intently over her choices. It was whilst we were purchasing his welcome home and Christmas presents, that we began to bump into familiar friendly faces from our lives, our town, who wanted only the best for us, and who helped us feel, yes, I'm going to use that word, "normal" again.

On day six, Saturday, Cheryl came over with Sam so that he could see where we lived and where Tom would be living, and after a short stay Tom was left with us in his new home to be returned by us to Cheryl's so that we could put him to bed. On leaving Tom there on Saturday night Daisy broke down in the car outside Cheryl's house. She cried her heart out. It felt wrong, she felt sad and, 'Why couldn't

Tom come home to sleep? I don't want to leave him there.'

She went to bed later than she needed that night and in line with the introduction plan we had to wake her at 5.30 the next morning again in order to be back at Cheryl's for 7am. Daisy was exhausted. We had all come down with colds and were worn out from an emotional rollercoaster of a week.

So on that Sunday morning, at 7am as agreed, we woke Tom up and brought him home after giving him breakfast at Cheryl's, only to have a meeting with Aggie and then drive him back to Cheryl's a mere four hours after waking him up. It was our shortest time with him since the first day. And all because Cheryl's family had wanted to have a goodbye party, which apparently, absolutely, had to take place all afternoon and evening and we were expected to ferry him back on demand. We had questioned the wisdom of this prolonged goodbye earlier in the week but were told that regardless of its merit it was to happen. We had understood that the intention of the week was to increase Tom's time with us to enable a smooth transition on that final Monday morning, and yet the end of the week seemed to undo all progress. It was hard to see the wisdom of a baby spending almost his entire last day back in the bosom of the family he was unknowingly to be taken from for good the very next morning.

We had realised that our thoughts and opinions were merely being noted as such and not addressed, and so had stepped up our own progress in the second half of the week. During one of our unscheduled visits home we briefly introduced Tom to both sets of his grandparents. Two days later they were to begin a pivotal, key part in his life, and would be a constant presence for him, and right then it was exactly what we needed, some good old fashioned moral support.

It was good to see Aggie that Sunday. We made it known that the week had not worked in Tom's or our interests and that we felt children's services should have supported the foster carer rather than making her needs the priority. As usual we took Tom back on time. Daisy's time with him that Sunday was spent either in the car or in the presence of Aggie who, lovely as she is, was Daisy's embodiment of children's services. It was unacceptable.

The next morning the three of us woke early again to travel over to Cheryl's house where the attendees of the planning meeting were to reconvene, review the week and then, all being well, send us on our way. Daisy sat politely frozen through a meeting that the social workers kept their coats on for, so cold was it in Cheryl's front room. Whilst Tom played on my lap, and with Sam at school, ten of us crowded into the tiny room and set about courteously reviewing the events of the week.

Knowing full well the grief Cheryl was enduring, James and I had agreed not to raise any problems on the very morning Cheryl was to have to say goodbye to Tom. We wanted to make constructive suggestions to aid future adopters. We wanted to go home. And we did whatever we had to do to get home as a family as quickly as was possible. An hour and a bit later, that was exactly where we were headed. The four of us.

Though there was no preparing Daisy for the moment itself. Cheryl sobbed as I handed her a bouquet of flowers and a gift for Sam. Then, also crying, I hugged her by way of apology for being the baby thief I had been made to feel. And Daisy? She looked on, expressionless, while children's services, for Tom's records, photographed our taking Tom, leaving Cheryl's house, walking down the road to the car and driving off. It was surreal and incredibly unsettling. Quiet. Too quiet. Cheryl's front door closed. It was supposed to be a happy moment for a six-year-old girl and yet she can't honestly say that it was.

As we turned the corner we breathed easily for perhaps the first time in seven days, but it would take more than that to expel all the pent-up emotions we had been keeping in. It took a long time for things to feel right again and the problem wasn't Tom: it was getting him. The impact this made on Daisy's life took us into Christmas and beyond.

There was no two-week adoption leave for Daisy. It was back to school, and what she would have done without the normality of her lovely teacher and best friend, I do not know.

'We're never going to see Cheryl again, are we, Mum?' No. It was Cheryl's request at first, indeed her opening statement at the planning meeting: 'I can't see him again once he's gone.' And now it would also be our decision. We would not be seeing Cheryl again. Sad but true. Daisy had been left out, hadn't slept well, hadn't seen enough of her parents, and hadn't lived properly for one long week. She had, however, been made to feel that she had stolen someone else's baby.

The day after Mother's Day, some four months later, we had a phone call from children's services. It was about Cheryl. She had been in touch. Mother's Day had proved too much and she wanted to see Tom. Our answer was "no" and both Jo and Aggie agreed. Not for the first time we had to reassure Daisy that Tom had a birth mother, Sarah, and a mother, me, and that Cheryl was a foster carer whom Tom simply would not remember in years to come and whom she, Daisy, never had to see again. Daisy wanted confirmation: 'She has gone though, Mummy, hasn't she? She's not going to just turn up?' James and I looked at one another. We got Daisy into this and we were sure as hell going to get her out of it.

Though not on the market at that time, or even ready to sell, we moved house only twelve weeks later and instructed children's services not to pass on our new details to Cheryl. It was not the sole reason for our move but the most important one. We were ready for a fresh start, a real one this time, though we stayed local and we were doing it as a family of four.

We will never forget the love that Cheryl and her son showed to our son and are thankful to her for that. She would have benefited from more guidance and support and to her credit she has, I understand, elected not to foster any more babies; a little too late for Daisy and Sam, for whom this had been an unforgettable experience. And though no danger to us, Cheryl had tainted our start together as a family, but she is not the only, or last, mother to put her own child and her own needs before those of another. I am now unrepentantly guilty of that too. For if I don't put Daisy first, no one else will.

And so we lifted up our heads and walked straight into Christmas. 'How lovely,' people said, 'And at this time of year too. You must be so happy,' and we should have been. Really we were. With only weeks to Christmas Day we had more than we had ever dared hope for – our very own miracle, one special baby boy.

When we walked in through our own front door on that last day of the introductions, a "New Baby Boy" banner adorning it for all to see courtesy of my very proud parents, holding Tom on the cusp of our new life together as a family, James disappeared into the kitchen and stayed there a good ten minutes or so whilst he cried and cried like I have never before and never again seen him cry.

5

The spectacle of adoption

Most, if not all, new parents are familiar with the attention, fuss and fluffy stuff that a newborn baby can elicit from others. That well-intentioned gush of warmth, that in all probability, we would be rather offended not to experience. Having been lucky enough both to give birth to and to adopt a baby, I think I can say that the reaction after Daisy's birth, and she did prompt a decidedly pink outburst of coochy-coo noise wherever she went, was nothing, nothing whatsoever, compared with the impact made by Tom's arrival.

This was the second thing that we had not been prepared for, the first being the rather dark hole we had found ourselves in during introductions. It is a credit to the people in our lives, and I'm not talking about family or close friends here but alluding to the wider community around us, that Tom's arrival heralded a new world record in "attention receiving". Well, OK, maybe not a world record but it was pretty intense. Possibly it was more impressive as it occured at precisely the same time as a national scandal involving the fatal neglect of a baby boy. A shocked nation consumed the shameful details as they surfaced, triggering in their wake the upheaval and investigation of children's services up and down the country. It was a particularly sad and devastating reality when told against the backdrop of the season's customary festive goodwill, and it was perhaps obvious with hindsight that emotions and feelings would be heightened by the arrival of a baby boy previously "in care". Much of adoption is such a very private, inwardly searching affair that we were about as unprepared as you could be for this.

For us it was time for Christmas: the school nativity play was in rehearsal, costumes had to be provided – no mean feat considering Daisy had been cast as a hailstone – and what we wanted was to immerse ourselves in tinsel and fairy lights. But we forgot one thing: overnight, somewhat miraculously, there we were, for all to see, with our new baby boy. "Baby Jesus," Daisy joked at home with us. Everybody loves a happy ending and we were it. For some people, it was more about them than us. I understand that for I think I'd have been the same.

I mean this a little flippantly I'll admit, but it became obvious during our journey to adopt that many of the residents of our home town had always wanted to adopt, would like to do so one day, may still do so. 'You never know,' they said and there were all those who knew someone who was 'actually adopted, you know'. That is, of course, all except those who 'couldn't do that', who couldn't possibly 'love someone else's child.' And so began a new relationship with humankind: one of spectacle and comment.

Let me quickly point out that without this warmth, this freedom to speak their minds to us and demonstrate their feelings, it would not be home. We would have been worried. And what we appreciated more than anything right then was our home town. Not much gets past this lot – our lot. And the person who was honest enough to state that she wouldn't be able to do it, to have 'someone else's child,' was the first to say: 'he's one of us now'. Getting to know her as I have, I think she's a lovely mum and a strong lady to boot, and I think if a child were brought to her door she would feel differently. Not that this would happen, and I know she would never consider adoption an option. I used to believe that if you thought the way she did, then you couldn't possibly do it, for Tom is not "someone else's" child. But, as with many things in life, until you are put in a situation or indeed put yourself in one, it is often impossible to envisage doing something, and never more so than contemplating adoption after having given birth to your own flesh and blood. How could it possibly compare? This lady hadn't ever had, or had to have, that whole 'It's not the pregnancy bit that matters' moment. It took us long enough.

Many people like to entertain the idea of adoption but few actively pursue it, most because they do not ever have to. I am no longer offended when someone says, 'I couldn't do it,' as if it were the bronze medal, with pregnancy taking gold and fertility treatment snatching the silver, for it is not for everyone.

By becoming adopters we are still very much in a minority out there and so have joined those that "do" as a source of fascination for others. Our life and Daisy's brother, felt for a good while like public property.

Much of this attention was borne out of love alone, for instance, I would pop out on some errand or other and bump into someone familiar and before I knew what was happening a grown man could be hugging me as if his life depended on it. I had bouquets of flowers given to me and bucketsful of tears. I'm not for one moment complaining but rather trying to explain how unprepared we had been for this level of intensity, which on an individual basis was perfectly touching but became very, very overwhelming en masse. Some days it felt like being a bride on her wedding day trying to make a beeline for the toilets. It would take forever to get there. There was always someone to talk to, always someone who deserved your time and thanks, for we had been wonderfully supported throughout.

However, we had been through many stages over three years, many landmarks, many hurdles and I guess, happy as we were, we were just desperate to get on with real life: practical life, family life.

To Daisy this was all a bit of a snowball from the blue that quickly gathered both momentum and size before she even saw it coming. It never hit her. It landed just to her right but she still got sprayed with snow from the impact. The day after we brought Tom home we chose to send Daisy to school. We wanted her to have some normality after the abnormal existence of the previous week and for her to be involved in the exciting, uplifting festive cheer that the end of the Christmas term generates, and of course, there were her nativity play rehearsals. Daisy's teacher, Mrs Street, whom she was lucky enough to have for two consecutive years, was a welcome constant for Daisy in what were unsettling times. She was utterly brilliant at asking Daisy about her future brother or sister in the same way she did when new baby siblings were born into classmates' families. Mrs Street helped to normalise adoption a little more for Daisy and for her friends. And so, before we'd had time to experience the reaction that was to come and because it is the tight knit little school that it is, we thought nothing of popping in with Tom on the first morning back at school to see Mrs Street. This was done with the sole purpose of showing him off and to give Daisy the moment that many of her classmates had enjoyed. She had waited long enough and incredibly patiently for her moment. Yes, we could have chosen not to wheel him out in front of Daisy's class but unacknowledged at birth, we wanted him to have the fuss that should always have been his. And we wanted to show him off as much as the next new parents. Daisy herself wanted us to.

It had been suggested by the social workers that it would also be nice to take Tom to pick Daisy up at the end of school that day. When push came to shove, Daisy couldn't get anywhere near us. This pasty, worn out looking small child stood on the outskirts of fifteen or so well wishers and onlookers who were all so busy saying such lovely things and wanting to see Tom, to show an interest, that they didn't notice her there. We were more or less the last to leave the school playground that afternoon and Daisy was the last to get close to Tom. She didn't hold it against him. She didn't say much really, which was not, is not, like her. Not like the Daisy we know and love.

I do remember saying to James the next morning, 'Shall I stay at home with Tom and you take Daisy to school?' But we all went. Daisy wouldn't have it any other way.

I wish I could say the attention stopped then. It did die down eventually but it took months and months for it to fade and now we just get the occasional 'How's it going?' which is like asking Daisy how she's settling in. It felt just a tiny bit for a while like we might be part of some local social experiment.

But they didn't all crowd round. One person in particular didn't come anywhere near us, didn't acknowledge Tom for about four weeks, and then suddenly one day she walked up to me and asked me outright: 'What happened to his real mum, then?' Lots of people wanted to know, and some of them would apologise for asking; again, I can relate to their curiosity.

There was definitely an element of disbelief that Tom could be so gorgeous. No one meant anything negative by this and I do understand their disbelief that so charming and cute a child could be up for adoption in the first place. 'Why wouldn't he be any of those things?' is the logical question, but I'm sorry, Tom, I remember when I went on my own to an adoption support group meeting where I met adopters and their children, that I couldn't believe how truly gorgeous the children were. All of them adopted. I remember reporting this back to James as if it were newsworthy or had ever been in dispute. So what does that say about me? I think that the publicity surrounding adoption is largely responsible. There are certainly a great number of beautiful children out there who have severe disabilities, and it is often these "harder to place" children that the general public sees promoted as being "up" for adoption. This is a necessary reality check for anyone who has a romantic notion about adoption, but it is not what the average person is prepared to choose to take on. To opt to adopt back-breaking responsibilities, lifelong struggles on behalf of such a child, no matter how gorgeous, is for many unthinkable, particularly so if they already have children.

Although these harder to place children do need more publicity, often the children that end up in care have suffered more from neglect and abuse than anything else. They may, of course, have huge attachment and behavioural issues that can be as daunting as disability to address. A great many people think that no one would give up, could give up a healthy, attractive child, but the sad fact is that sometimes drug or alcohol misuse, domestic violence, serious illness or social misfortune can prevent a parent from caring for a child. It follows that we should not be surprised at how like any other child Tom was and is. Rages aside, it is plain to see that he is not a particularly challenging prospect, though of course there are days when I beg to differ. Yet it is, without doubt, a shock for people to know that Tom is not only adopted but was given away by his own birth mother.

That said, I am a huge supporter, sometimes I feel defender would be more apt, of Sarah though she will in all likelihood never know this. Of everyone in "Tom's Tale", she comes out of it the worst. The first week we brought Tom home, James and I took him to the doctor to have his chesty cough investigated. Throughout our appointment the doctor, despite knowing absolutely nothing about Tom's birth mother, talked dismissively and negatively in front of Tom about her: 'You know what these birth mothers are like,' he began. Though Tom was too young at the time to understand, I wanted to cover his ears and to defend Sarah. I did neither, caught off guard, but I've learnt quickly.

James and I are adamant never to paint Sarah any way other than fairly and as positively as possible. She gave us Tom, the most precious gift, and without her we wouldn't be the family we are. We have read that Sarah, as a result of her actions, has been on the receiving end of some hurtful and unnecessary vilification from some members within her community and it pains us to know this. We ourselves have encountered a little of the brush she has been tarred with: many assume she is some young drug addict; she is not. She made a decision, and probably before that a mistake, and did the best she could by the unwanted child she conceived.

Was it the very fact that we already had a child that made Tom's arrival so public? With no older child there would be no school. With no school there would be no playground and no parents. It is possible that we could have slipped Tom into our life a little more slowly, more gently maybe. There was never any chance of that. We were well and truly embedded in local life. Family and friends are everywhere. My much loved mother-in-law has been known to ring us up and say, 'Your curtains are still closed'; my dad, once a father, always a father, has rung to inform me that, 'A strange man has just walked through your front door.' To solve these mysteries... we had a lazy morning that particular day, and it was I who let the "strange man", Daisy's godfather Andy, in. This is a good place to bring up children and a lot of people return here after adventures further afield to do just that. Having Daisy made us an active part of the community. If Tom had been our first child, would we have had a quieter time of introducing him into our lives? Was Daisy's existence responsible for the spectacle that was Tom?

No. A child's sudden apperance, whether there is an older sibling or not, cannot go unnoticed. Questions would come from nowhere. I turned up to join a local "stay and play" group after a couple of months of bonding at home, and the older ladies who ran it were surprised we hadn't been before, considering Tom's age. They quizzed me on whether I'd just moved into the area, whether I hadn't fancied it until now, and if not why not? Resistance was futile. There, under the spotlight of the kitchen serving hatch, I told two complete strangers that I had adopted him, just to pay my pound and get my coffee and biscuit. Only very recently we stumbled into another situation where Tom's adoption was outed rather publicly, once again to complete strangers, and again arousing much interest. James and I were, rather mundanely we thought, attempting to change Tom's building society account to his new surname in order to pay money in. It quickly became apparent that this was not a common procedure for them and there was much checking to be done and a phone call to be made. They couldn't have been nicer to us but you could feel all the other customers perk up to listen in for more snippets, and as ever Tom got that sudden injection of attention reserved for adopted children.

So perhaps expect a little more attention along the way than may feel comfortable when you adopt and are merely intent on going about your day-to-day business. It does die down. We really aren't that interesting. By and large Tom is old news now. We've done most of our "firsts".

We'll never opt to see the doctor again who badmouthed Sarah; but the person who was so seemingly unimpressed with Tom that they gave him a wide berth for a whole month is actually particularly lovely to him now in a perfectly humdrum, day-to-day kind of way. As for everyone else? They celebrated for us, they made us feel like they cared, and now I think Tom is just Tom to them, which is the single greatest thing that they could ever do for him or any adopted child. The only spectacle surrounding him now is the one he tends to make of himself.

Tom is busy stamping his personality on the world and it is Daisy who has to put up with his tantrums or his stealing the limelight: like the time during the celebratory achievement assembly that they have every Friday at Daisy's school, when he shouted, 'Uh oh,' and left the entire school in fits of giggles and doing impersonations of Daisy's baby brother whilst poor Mr Miller, the Head, struggled to regain their attention. Then there is his triumphant 'Goal' shouted at inopportune moments, such as the two-minute silence on Remembrance Day when we attended to watch Daisy parade as a Brownie, or when he makes passers-by laugh out loud or panic because he is arching out of his pushchair, like the actress, Kate Winslet, arches out from the deck of the Titanic, as we make our way back home down the steep hill after school. None of which has anything to do with his being adopted.

I was laughing about Tom's antics with Daisy the other day when she said, 'What about the wedding, Mum?' My reply was a quick, 'Which one?' The one where he blew raspberries all through the wedding vows, completely upstaging Daisy as a bridesmaid, never mind the would-be newlyweds; or the one where he said, 'Oh no,' very loudly when the vicar asked if anyone objected to the wedding? Luckily Daisy finds all this hilarious and perhaps the age gap has helped here.

Laughing aside, it was really hard for Daisy at times. Not that she has been knowingly left out; several people gave her some very thoughtful cards and presents when Tom first came on the scene, and of course, being the recipient of a few gifts helped along the way. Not to mention the BIG SISTER T-shirt from best friend Holly; thanks Holly. But it was hard because the last thing that Daisy ever wanted in her young life was a whole lot of attention. Her favourite quote from a well known Disney phenomenon is, 'Why is everyone staring at me?' She even gets coy entering the lounge on Christmas Day to see if Father Christmas has left her any presents.

Though change may be afoot, for Daisy has informed me that one of her aims in life is, 'To have my picture on my lunchbox'. Persistent little songwriter and rock chick in the making that she is, I don't want to discourage her for a moment, but couldn't help suggesting that perhaps she should aim to pay for her own lunch box first and then maybe also some lunch to go in it. Although this marketing savvy may well be a sign of the times, it struck me that this latest turn of ambition showed that becoming public property for the first few months after we brought Tom home can't have done Daisy that much harm, can't have caused any lasting damage. Even I wouldn't dare compare the people of our lovely home town to the paparazzi – now that would be ungrateful. After all, no one ever actually photographed Tom; we never actually even made the local newspaper.

When it comes to adopting a child, a sense of humour is utterly essential at all times. Something existing parents should have enough experience in, but it is a lot more to ask of a child. Isn't it, Daisy?

'Daisy, what do you think? Have we had to laugh a lot about what other people do and say about Tom?'

'Can I have a snack?' she asks. And there it is, that little slice of normality I was craving a year ago.

6

Who knows what?

I have made no secret that, at times, we have found it surprisingly difficult to adhere to the well intentioned guidelines we gave ourselves in order to maintain both integrity and privacy on behalf of Tom. Perhaps it is a case of who *should* know what, rather than who actually does happen to know.

It struck us that the only person who should know everything about Tom's adoption apart from ourselves was Tom. This is his life, after all. In its entirety, his life encompasses matters reaching far into a past that is not our past. The information that was so important to us when we were first approached about a match with Tom will increase in weight and relevance as Tom takes rightful ownership of it. What right or need does anyone else have to know anything of it? None, in theory. In practice it has been a little different.

Tom will grow up like most adopted children today, with an understanding of exactly what led to his adoption. Or at the very least, what is known to have led to it. Therefore in a family of four, with the upfront and honest approach to adoption that is now encouraged, it naturally follows that there is one other who will be unable to escape the realities of Tom's beginning, and that is Daisy.

Given that Tom was one of the youngest babies ever placed for adoption by our local authority, it also follows that Daisy knows a whole lot more about his adoption, at this stage of their lives, than Tom does. So we find ourselves in the rather outdated position of having to break the news to Tom that he is adopted. Though by using his infancy to his advantage, and gradually feeding him the facts of his life, he will be spared the sudden shock of revelation experienced by so many adopted children in years gone by. One day soon, when his language and understanding skills have improved (he is currently twenty months old), we will need to start dropping into his little world the very idea of adoption, and that he himself is adopted.

Daisy has the dubious privilege of being the oldest child by six years. When the sibling of an adopted child is significantly older, what does that mean in regards to who knows what? We felt Daisy needed to know a little of Tom's history in order for her to enter into his adoption without mystery and speculation. There is an element of risk here but we hope and trust that we can rely on her not to take away in one sibling spat all that Tom holds dear from his childhood, like Father Christmas and the Tooth Fairy, who both, I am glad to say, still visit our house and look set to do so for a good while yet. As Daisy roams through the next few years on her intrepid exploration from junior to secondary school we will encourage and guide her to do the right thing by Tom; to let him take his time understanding what it is he is being told and how it may differ from so many of his friends' experiences without the upset of an overwhelming, sudden outburst from a rather wound up big sister. Having been one myself, I know just how well a younger sibling knows which buttons to press.

I have little doubt that Daisy will revel in the chance to keep all Tom's plates spinning with the childhood beliefs that she herself has so enjoyed, and do not think she would ever whip anything from underneath him out of spite. However, many a rash act is carried out in the heat of the moment, so it is a huge responsibility for Daisy never to hold Tom's adoption over him; never to use the fact that she is our birth child to differentiate herself from Tom, or to tease him with any details about his background. Consequently, it was with a great deal of thought that we shared some of Tom's pre-adoption history with her.

For Daisy's sake, it was imperative to comb through the detail of Tom's life, extracting all the palatable, age-appropriate bits that would put a stop to wild imagination and fear. So what does she know? She knows that Tom has an older half-brother, Kyle, who is a couple of years younger than she is. She has seen a photograph of Kyle, several of Sarah and various ones of other extended family members whom she can't recall by name. We have told Daisy that Sarah was not happy enough, did not feel able to look after Tom because she did not have the support of Tom's birth father. She also knows that Tom went to live with Cheryl, the foster carer, soon after he was born. It was important for us to see how Daisy coped with this information.

After the shocking discovery of children without parents, and adoption as an option, Daisy's world accommodated, as best it could, the idea of a mother giving away her baby; not just any baby, but Daisy's very own, beloved, much longed for, baby brother. It is understandable that despite our editing out the highlights, this continues to confound her. We hear it referred to every now and again. It still churns round in her mind. But then it would, wouldn't it? Adults struggle. I can see it in the way they shake their heads when they watch him tottering around being so utterly adorable. If you met him you'd think the same: 'How could she?' So you can imagine what Daisy made of it all. And it just hangs there in the air waiting for her to grow up just a little bit more.

So far, Daisy has asked for little else in the way of facts. Tom's life history box is not out of bounds to her and she can look at it with supervision, if she asks. I think right now she simply doesn't require any further information. On a day-to-day basis Daisy feels she knows everything there is to know about Tom and this is exactly how she handles the subject with her friends. She has long since clarified his status as her brother with them and patiently replied in the early days to questions such as 'Is he your real brother?' with a polite 'Yes'. And then the 'But he didn't come out of your mummy's tummy' sometimes followed by the 'Is he your half-brother?' with a skilful 'He's my whole brother. He's just adopted. It's just how we got him.' Daisy's friends never ask her for any detail of his life story for they are all too busy with their own lives. The key fact is enough for them to entertain.

And this is exactly what we will be doing for Tom: selecting key snippets of his life story pre-us. I dipped my toe in quite unexpectedly a few months ago when leafing through his life history box. He trundled over to me, grinning as he invariably is, and stopped to see what I was looking at. It was a large A4 print of Sarah holding Tom in hospital. The only way to start gently drip-feeding it in, I thought, without James there to confer with, is to start gently drip-feeding it in. And so it began: 'This is your birth mother, Tom,' I said. 'Look, she's holding baby Tom.' He looked at me and then back at the photo. 'She's pretty isn't she?' I smiled. 'Ahhh,' he said, putting both hands out and touching her. And then he lay his head down on the photo just like he does when he nuzzles Einstein, the dog. Maybe he would have done that whoever was in the photograph, maybe it was the gentle, encouraging tone of my voice. Maybe. Whatever the truth, I thought it an amazing moment, a start, and it made me feel just that little bit more protective of Sarah and Tom. It is my job as Tom's mother to nurture and keep open any possibility of communication between the two, for both their sakes. What Tom decides as he grows up and matures is up to him, but I have promised myself never to do anything other than support him in his journey.

And that is exactly what this is. It is a journey for all of us, and "the box" and all it contains is pivotal when considering who knows what about that journey. It is easy to get preoccupied with who else should, or rather should not, know its contents. And I realised in the days after Tom came to live with us, that though there was a reasonable amount of documentation for him about his journey to us, there was nothing about ours to him. If this open approach to adoption was all about Tom accessing information to help him understand, then one thing was clear: James and I knew our story, Daisy had her version of events, but what about Tom? I wanted him to know the other side of his own story: what it was that had led us to him and how we had felt about having him. Perhaps he would never want to have the big sit down chat that might prove rather too emotional to handle on top of everything else he would have to confront. If that were the case or if anything ever happened to us, who would say how we felt about adopting Tom?

So I contributed to "the box" a few months ago. There are some very private things I wish to tell him one day, but they are to stay exactly that, for some things really are just for his ears and eyes only. However, there is an envelope that contains what was almost a cathartic exercise for me. On the envelope is written 'For Tom, Love Mum X'. It's for when he is older and, yes, it is soppy stuff but then I am allowed. I am his mother after all, and I will happily leave the silent understanding to Tom and his dad and the factual recording to children's services.

My letter to Tom is called "Slow Boat to Australia", which I think very apt. When we received our preparation group folder, a story of a journey was tucked discreetly away at the back. It uses the idea of travelling to a foreign destination by boat when everyone else around you seems to be flying there by aeroplane much more quickly and perhaps more easily, as a metaphor for adopting a child rather than conceiving one. My letter to Tom uses the same metaphor to explain my feelings about having a child by both means. I hope it also sums up my feelings about introducing adoption as an option to James and Daisy, the innocent part Tom played in it, our journey, and perhaps my concerns too. This is what it says:

> *Every now and again I ask your dad, 'Are we nearly there yet?' He tends to ply me with chocolate or wine, I'm partial to both, and we keep on going. Home. I carry a precious cargo as I go. You three and a box. A perfectly innocent looking box, and yet inside waiting for me to drip-feed to you, Tom, my beautiful baby boy, is the fact that will remain at your very core. Once upon a time you belonged to someone else. The adoption process is like taking a slow boat to Australia when women all around are pregnant and flying there first class. Well I've flown first class with your gorgeous big sister, and I've taken the slow boat with you, and I can honestly say both journeys are rich beyond imagining.*
>
> *I set us sailing on this epic adventure, but like Dorothy in the Wizard of Oz, I can safely say, 'There is no place like home,' and short of clicking my ruby slippers together that is exactly where I am taking us now. The Scarecrow, Tin Man, and Cowardly Lion have nothing on you three. Better companions or crew I could not have wished for and yet our travels are far from over. As the years go by, and the contents of that box sink in, you will be embarking on a challenging stage of your life's journey, and our passports will never be away for long. In years to come when you turn round and tell me that you hate me and that I am not your*

real mother anyway, I'll open my passport and remind myself of how far we've come.

I'm a seasoned traveller, I travel well. Take aim at me in anger and confusion, should you need to, but please be gentle with your sister who, herself only a child, has a love for you so humbling to watch, your dad, who came on board at first out of love for me but who fell wonderfully in love with you, and your doting grandparents, so proud to have their first ever grandson.

That first night, when I held you as you cried, I knew exactly how it was. I am your mother. My journey to find you has been both the stretch marks of pregnancy and the pain of childbirth. You are every inch ours. But I want you to know something. In all the years of searching and waiting for you the one thing that brought me to my knees was that photo, provided by your birth maternal grandmother, of your birth mother as a child. She looked like you do and so very, very happy, Tom. Her life changed that. Changed her. Happiness is vulnerable and not to be taken for granted. I fully understand the purpose of the photo. We all travel as best we can through life, Tom. We four have each other and more. Not everyone is that lucky. I'm just glad I was there to catch you as you fell, that's what mums try to do, slow boat or otherwise.

I have not read this letter to Daisy but when she is old enough she will have access to it should she wish. As Daisy's mother I try to protect her and spare her from dwelling on, going over, the journey we have made together to get to where we are now. She's so happy and enjoying life to the full and, since she has no issues with what we have done as a family, I do not think it wise to make any, if not necessary. I have, however, told her repeatedly how very proud her father and I are of the way in which she has embraced the whole process of adoption. We will be here and ready, should she decide she does need more in the way of information or reassurance.

As for myself, I don't look in "the box" very often for we feel it is Tom's to share with us, or not, once he is old enough to know, to decide, but very soon we shall have to make a point of delving in there with him to introduce him to it. I suppose that Daisy is right. We feel as she does. Until matters arise that need addressing, Tom's history pre-adoption has little relevance to our daily family life. I have toyed with the idea of asking Daisy to write something down about how she feels right now about Tom's adoption so that it can be stored for future posterity: to show him just how over the moon she was at his arrival, because these things can be hard to say, hard to bring up in conversation when people are busy just getting on with life. But I have yet to suggest it, for I can almost hear her reply. 'Why?'

Daisy doesn't volunteer that Tom is adopted. She purposefully left his adoption off the family tree she had to produce at the infant school, and she has no desire for any of her teachers at her new junior school to know. It is not a secret, just not something she wishes to be brought up. What relevance could it possibly have? This has nothing to do with embarrassment or shame. Daisy is living the here and now. For her it is simple.

James and I are practising not to mention the fact that Tom is adopted. Day to day, it doesn't tend to crop up any more. But there are random questions that come out of the blue and catch you off guard. Last summer, at a wedding, we were enjoying a laugh and chat with someone we had never met before, a mother of a little boy who is almost the same age as Tom, and she asked a simple question: 'When's his birthday, then?' James' momentary hesitation and stumbling, and his enquiring look to me caught her attention straight away, though if she had known James, she would have thought this quite typical of him. 'The 2nd,' I chipped in, with such certainty that I instantly doubted myself, 'Er the 2nd? Yes, the 2nd.' I nearly caught myself out for it simply was not, at that time, as ingrained in my mind as perhaps the date that we brought him home was. We laughed it off, and resisted explaining away our shameful pause.

It is at moments like this when it can all too easily come spilling out of my mouth. I have found that it tends to happen when I am talking to another mother and it sometimes feels as if I am fending off a question yet to be asked. Only last week, on a bit of a roll, I managed to tell two mothers in two separate instances that Tom was adopted, and with hindsight I'm sure I could have avoided doing so on both occasions. It doesn't matter right now, but I get very cross with myself and wonder why I have not yet mastered the art. Tom's adoption is not my badge of honour and he does not need explaining away. There is nothing to hide, yet there are times when it feels as if the "telling" may be the result of a cocktail of bursting pride and burdening secrecy. The intention not to mention Tom's adoption in a way conflicts with the open policy that has replaced the pressure of the secretive days, when it was all very much a hush-hush "bombshell in the making" sort of affair. The line between proud parent and privacy can be a fine line to tread.

It is our belief that Tom does not need to grow up with the constant reminder that he was adopted. He will not want the sympathetic looks he currently gets from those who are unable as yet to get it out of their minds. We are very happy being open and upfront but Tom's privacy must come first. Getting this right every time is becoming easier but it has been a surprising challenge.

Nobody, apart from children's services, James and me, has seen the full contents of "the box" and in all probability this is precisely the way it will stay until perhaps the day Tom chooses to show a partner, and maybe later still, his children. It should go without saying that our family and close friends know a reasonable amount about Tom's history, though not all of them have asked for much detail. Some have asked nothing at all, whilst others ask freely, and neither is right or wrong. It is completely natural to wish to know as much as possible about the little boy they love, and of course it would be altogether too unlike us to have a mysterious family member in our midst. Tom doesn't do mystery. He's a straight in, bang it over the head kind of guy. We asked a lot of our family because adoption was new territory for them all, and they could not know for sure how they would actually feel on Tom's arrival. They could only hope to fall in love with him and they deserved to know more than the other peripheral people in our lives.

Outside of family, friends and friendly faces, there are institutions that need to be aware of the fact that Tom is adopted. I am led to understand that we should inform his school, when he is old enough to attend, in order that his teacher can be aware. The topic could pop up in discussions in the classroom or in the playground. Childhood may be magical but it can also be rather brutal and to the point. There is very little regard for political correctness in the playground, and Prime Minister's Question Time has nothing on the inquisition a six-year-old can subject you to. So here it is a case of forewarned is forearmed. Though watching Daisy in action, I am sure that Tom will also conduct himself far more confidently than perhaps we have to date.

There have been several occasions when Tom's adoption has been highlighted out of legal and medical necessity, for instance, changing names on Tom's bank account and registering him with the doctor. In general, professional people are a little more circumspect and do not probe further. As yet, we have not been in a situation where his birth family medical history has been relevant. Children's services ensured that we knew all that they themselves were aware of medically, but the time will probably come when we are asked questions about Tom's heredity that will bring adoption to the fore.

I think it would be fair to conclude that the answer to the question in this chapter's title will change with time. Eventually it should really only be answered by Tom. But I have just remembered something Aggie, our social worker, said to us at the very beginning: only time will tell how this open approach to adoption has worked. She's right, only time will reveal what effect it will have on those adopted and those close to them. I guess, as with all parenting, it comes down to trial and error. I wonder what Tom will be saying to us in twenty years' time?

7

The definition of family

This morning when Daisy said, 'What have they got to do with us?' I laughed, only because I knew before I even asked her, how she felt about Tom's birth family and what she would say. She elaborated on what could have seemed a rather ignorant remark: 'Mum, a family is when you belong together and do things together.' So there you go, that is Daisy's definition of family, and Tom's birth relatives do not conform.

Yesterday I discovered that there are nine definitions of the word "family" in my dictionary. All nine of them involve a group and the sense of belonging. Daisy counts family as people she cares for, who care for her and who have connections to her life today. Cut off and thrust away from his birth family, Tom's belonging to them is difficult to entertain, certainly impossible to visualise, and for Daisy downright ridiculous to believe. There is nothing tangible to tie Tom's birth family to him, let alone to Daisy, and therefore qualify them as family. The fact that they exist is not relevant here. However, they do exist and out there somewhere they most certainly are.

With this in mind, I pushed her a little further on how

she felt about this invisible birth family of Tom's. 'Sad,' she said. 'Really?' I asked, wondering who it was she felt sad for.

'Yes, it's not nice for Tom that he doesn't know them. He needs to know about them. He needs to meet them one day so that he can fit them in.'

You don't have to be Daisy's mother to know that it would unnerve her a little if Tom did have direct contact with them, and I am ready to admit that it is not something we would have wished for, though we certainly would have endorsed it, had it been deemed appropriate or desirable or even mentioned for that matter. It is upsetting to think that Tom will have to digest the fact that this supposed family of his chose to have no further contact with him, and entrusted him to a system they hoped would ensure he received adequate care.

Possibly, when Tom nears the end of childhood, this situation may change.

'So what would you feel if, probably when, he does decide to attempt to meet with them?' I asked Daisy "casually", reversing out of the drive as if it were neither here nor there how she truly felt.

'Glad for him,' she said and then added a little defensively, 'Anyway, they don't feel or act like a family should'.

And she's right, they have not made it easy for Tom to connect with them. Sarah chose neither to write him her own letter to reveal her feelings and reasons for parting with him, nor to have any letterbox contact with him over the future years. If family means a sense of belonging to a unit or group of people, then Daisy is right: they simply do not fit the bill. Until the day Tom chooses to meet them, if indeed he ever does, they remain strangers and to Daisy that is a shame but a fact.

There is evidence of Daisy grappling with a new level of understanding: 'I know Sarah didn't feel she could look after Tom and be happy, Mum. We are all different.' I smile at the parrot fashion repetition of my own effort at reasoning. I am pleased that, despite her strength of love for Tom and her deep down disgust that Sarah could part with him in the first place, Daisy has tried, at such a very young age, to show empathy and to embrace a positive, honest standpoint. I commend her for that.

But it is impossible not to note that Daisy wastes no time in stripping bare Tom's other family of any semblance of a romantic notion. They are his family by blood and blood alone, and could perhaps one day be "allowed" to have a relationship with Tom if he so chooses. But for Daisy, family is a commitment. I cannot argue with her for deep down I agree. I did remind her that they always will be Tom's birth family. But I also let her know that I thought she was right, and that I would wish my children to feel as she does about being in a family.

With that in mind, now that it feels like Tom has always been with us, where does this "family" of his begin and end? Rights and wrongs aside, is there *any* connection between adoption and birth? It sadly doesn't take any soul searching to come up with the answer. Hardly any. My thoughts of any connection with them are fuelled by love of Tom alone. I wish to preserve any shred of a link between them and Tom so that he has the best shot, and his rightful chance, to address any issues he has regarding them in the future. As for me, I was offered the most precious gift of all because of the vagaries of their family life, or the lack of it, and for that reason alone I am tied to them. We may never meet, yet it feels as if the blurred line between my family and theirs will be forever there.

Although Daisy is quite clear about the divide between Sarah and co. and Tom and herself, there have been moments when it must have felt to her as if they were members of our extended family: long distant relatives capable of touching our lives and having significant impact on it without notice. Like the time we received a phonecall from Tom's social worker, Jo, quite unexpectedly one day last year shortly before Tom's final court hearing. She simply said: 'I've got some news. It's about Sarah. I've just been called to a meeting about Sarah. There has been a development.'

With the adoption not yet complete I closed my eyes and bit down on my bottom lip as my stomach tensed, and everything Aggie had ever said about the risk of adopting a relinquished child flooded through my head. I was quick to panic. I thought of Daisy and what it would do to her if Tom had to be returned to Sarah. For us it would be as if our son had died. What would it do to him? Had we been complete fools to even consider Tom and expose him and ourselves to such heartbreak? How ferociously would we be able to fight to keep him? I felt momentarily like a wild animal protecting her young. But wouldn't it be a good thing for Tom? Shouldn't we want this for him? Despite knowing the risks, we had always been reassured by the competent and very lovely Jo that the possibility of Sarah changing her mind was negligible and probably non-existent. We had put our trust in her judgement. Fortunately the call was quite the opposite of anything quite as shocking as losing our Tom. We were right to believe in Jo. Tom was still all set to be legally ours. Jo brought tidings of an altogether different sort.

It turned out that Sarah had been concealing another pregnancy, though this time only for the first few months, and she had actively, independently sought medical assistance. Due to her history, children's services were notified. Apparently she wanted to keep this baby and had concealed it until she thought Tom's adoption was secure. She had conceived her new baby only weeks after relinquishing Tom, and insisted that she felt able to keep this child primarily because she knew who, in this case, the birth father was. The child, thankfully not deemed at risk, was to be monitored by social workers but nothing more.

Back at the ranch, however, we were left reeling and wondering how best we were going to explain this turn of events to Tom as he got older. How could he not see right through to the unfairness of it all? Especially if he takes after his sister with her no nonsense, straight talking ways. We were indignant that Sarah could do this to him, though we realised that Sarah's new baby was not meant to be any sort of personal insult to Tom. But it did spell out only one word: rejection.

Calming down a little, it was obvious to both James and me that there was perhaps an elephant in the room that no one had mentioned, and it wasn't our place to do anything about it other than help Tom in years to come to understand the power of grief and, perhaps, guilt.

We feel that parting with Tom must have left scars on Sarah, and perhaps this new baby was going to be, dare I say it, a rebound baby. One to keep. Daisy, elephant or not, took the news badly and I guess said what we were all thinking: 'How can she do this? Isn't Tom good enough for her? Why didn't she keep him?' It was a good chance for us to practise what we would say to Tom when the time came for him to hear it.

The news continued to hang over us as we waited to hear of the birth. We wanted to know whether Tom had a half-sister or another half-brother and, if possible, we wanted to know their name. Since it had been brought to our attention in the first place, we now wanted to make sure that we had the complete picture: we wanted the facts to add to his life history box. As it happened, the information didn't come and we had to go looking for it.

After waiting patiently for a couple of months following the due date of Sarah's baby, hoping, expecting, to hear from children's services, we made two phone calls to chase them up, and still we heard nothing. Understaffed and overworked, it was just not a priority for them, and while we understood their situation, it was clearly our duty to do right by Tom. However, we decided that it was something we were going to have to get used to: once Sarah was off the social worker's radar, it was unlikely we would find out about any other future babies.

Events took another interesting twist one night while I was fast asleep. James, on Facebook, impulsively typed in Sarah's name and decided to do a search. As soon as he clicked on the mouse, he had open access to her page with up-to-date photos and the all-important missing information. Startled, a little unnerved, he came and woke me straight away and together, both feeling ill at ease, we read about her latest boyfriend and her two children: Kyle and Amy. It was a baby girl. Tom had a half-sister.

James and I reasoned with one another that surely the message of this page was the very justification for Tom's adoption. It was all about her, living her life. At least she looked happy. She sounded carefree although she did allude to "troubled times" when apparently her friends, featured on the page, had stuck by her. We wondered if perhaps by that she was referring to Tom. Whatever reason she had for giving up Tom, she was not letting it hold her back. It seemed quite the opposite was true. It was weird, it was voyeuristic and to be frank, frightening. The power of the internet is never to be underestimated. Adoption had gone from being shrouded in secrecy to social networking in just one click.

Obviously, if Sarah was so easily traceable, then quite possibly so would other members of Tom's birth family be and of course, as he grew older, Tom himself. If handled with care and at the right time, could this be a good thing? I am sure there are many stories from reunited birth relatives that both support and argue against the virtues of global communication. Perhaps it would have been better if James had never typed her name. Perhaps she should have had the foresight to give herself some privacy and

Tom some respect. We did, however, have the information we wanted for him. Tom's half-sister Amy will, in all probability, prove to be the hardest of any of Sarah's children for Tom to acknowledge, due to their closeness in age. For us, it prompted the conversation so many adopters end up having.

Would we consider adopting a birth sibling of Tom's if we were approached? Well, would we? That conversation hung around for a while. It would be incredibly difficult to say 'no' though we have no reason, right now, to suppose that we might be asked. The knock-on implications for Daisy, as well as for Tom, provided an interesting debate until at long last we tired ourselves out and got back on track with the life we had been enjoying pre-phone call.

It is not only the new generation of Tom's birth family that has given us cause for thought. The gut wrenching moment I had when I thought we might be about to lose Tom or, at the very least, have a fight on our hands to keep him, brought it home to me how hard it must be for the many birth relatives who have little say in the adoption of a child. One of the most valued things to come out of the adoption was a letter we have for Tom when he is older, written by his birth maternal grandmother, Jean. It is in the shaky hand so typical of some grandparents and certainly reminiscent of my own, but the content reveals that it is the letter of a mother. It is a touchingly biased account and attempt to explain her daughter's decision to give Tom up. In it Jean talks of Tom and how she will be almost ninety when he is eighteen and how she hopes to still be alive, 'You can be sure I'll do my best, darling,' so that she can meet him should he want to. It describes how she said goodbye, how she loves him, thinks of him all the time and that she hopes he is happy with his family. It is signed: 'Your heartbroken Grandma Jean'.

It is my wish that Tom does meet Jean one day, before it is too late, and that they share even one more moment together. Perhaps she can then leave this world when the time comes, at peace about something that was seemingly out of her control, but that affected her life so deeply. Jean writes, 'I do not know you but I love you,' and I understand that, for I too fell in love with Tom when I did not know him. The bond Jean feels will always be there, whether or not it is realised on both sides in the future. Tom's birth family, though no part of our day-to-day lives, are irrefutably real.

Daisy hasn't read the letter from Jean. We feel very strongly that Tom must be the next person to read it and it is in any case unsuitable for a child. The relationship it holds will one day differentiate Daisy from Tom. I am more than happy to hold the letter back, away from their childhoods, so that it is not a burden for them, but it is there, waiting for them to address one day. It is at this point, if any, when Daisy and Tom's lives will separate a little. Jean is Tom's birth family, not Daisy's. For Tom, his birth family will become more real than at any point before and brother and sister will have to readjust and reshuffle. To balance this out, we are set on raising Daisy and Tom to be confident in their belief that: 'You may not have the same genes but you are cut from the same cloth.' It is the love that James and I have for them both that they share.

8

Adoption conversations

Early in December 2009, we celebrated our first anniversary: a whole year of us being a family of four. It amounted to nothing more than a little tea party with just the four of us invited, for in keeping with our thoughts on Tom's adoption, we feel that as he grows up he might not want to celebrate what makes him different from us in this way. That's not to say we're right – it's merely our instinct.

James and I will always be acutely aware of the importance of that date, but perhaps it is best for Tom not be made to feel "special" because of it. He has a birthday, after all. We would rather Tom was as absorbed with his birthday as Daisy and any other child. If it happens that, once old enough to understand, he would rather we openly celebrated the day he "came home", then we will be sure to do so: Daisy would not object. She loves a party.

She wholeheartedly threw herself into this first anniversary, but wasn't particularly won over by the reason for it all and asked at the table, in her straight-faced, straight-laced way, 'I forget, what are we celebrating again?' Though rarely without her dry sense of humour, I couldn't help thinking that she meant it. That it really hadn't rated with her: the date or the significance. Or was she blocking it out? Would she rather forget the exhausting events of a year ago? Did the knock-on effect still rumble on? I don't believe so.

We had ensured that our family anniversary was a low-key affair; is it possible that we had made it too low key? Did the lack of validation from family and friends undermine its importance to Daisy? All the people who were aware of the significance of the date had been happy, at our request, to leave us to it. I'd like to say it was a dignified occasion, but to date, eating with Tom is anything but. It was child friendly, yes, intimate, eventful and fun and as far as tea parties go not entirely dissimilar to the chimpanzee variety. But James and I did feel very contented and there was an air of jubilation. Our status as a family seemed somehow strengthened: we had no longer "just adopted".

Although it had been a truly monumental year in the story of our little family, it actually didn't feel that way. It was impossible not to note how quickly and easily it had slipped by. Would we be able to say the same for all those years to come? Our thoughts turned to the future and all it might hold. However, before we had a chance to dwell on the possibilities, we slid once more into Christmas. Now, in early March, like everyone else in our lives, we have only recently emerged from hibernation and are keen to get on with whatever this year holds for us. Tom is 22 months old; he'll be two in May. Shortly after that I'll be writing my second letterbox letter to Tom's birth mother. I'm thinking about it already. It strikes me just how much has changed in one year.

Last summer Daisy was curious about our participation in letterbox contact – a rather one-sided arrangement for the time being. Despite her wish for Tom to have 'all the answers to his questions' she did not like it one bit: 'Can't it just be normal?' she wanted to know. Writing to Tom's birth mother once a year obviously didn't conform to Daisy's notion of normal. We explained that for Tom, and so for us, this would now be normal. We did our best to persuade her that it was something nice, a positive action we could take to help him understand what had happened to him; that it might give him those pivotal answers she herself wanted him to have. Daisy wasn't convinced. Letterbox contact was a peculiar, perhaps unwelcome, interruption. She didn't complain further, didn't make a fuss. Her lack of interest in even discussing the letter was judgement enough. Nevertheless, we fulfilled our commitment and, though a difficult letter to start, managed to write a comprehensive yet light hearted and warm summary of Tom's first six months with us, hoping that we were bringing him to life for Sarah.

This year, conversely, Daisy is all for it. Her thoughts and feelings have evolved as her understanding and appreciation for the situation matures. I suspect I may even have to muscle my way through to the laptop and heavily edit her contribution to this year's letter. She's very definite. 'I want Tom to have contact with Sarah.' This is in such stark contrast to last year's reaction that I decided to call her bluff and ask how she thought she would really feel if Sarah made letterbox contact with him. 'Excited,' the enthusiastic answer came straight away. I'm not sure what I had expected her to say – was this what she thought we wanted to hear? So I asked for more. 'Why excited?' Daisy looked at me and something passed between us. A sort of, 'I get it, OK? I understand, Mum. Don't worry about me.' Daisy shrugged, 'Excited if she decided she should'. I nodded. This made sense. Daisy would find it reassuring if a "mother" who had given away her baby wanted to keep in touch. It would be a comfort to Daisy that Tom's birth mother cared enough about him to at least want to write to him once a year.

'Maybe she will write in the future,' she said hopefully.

I tended to wonder about this a lot myself: about the future. 'Maybe,' I replied, cramming a whole biscuit into my mouth and having a moody munch for suddenly, momentarily, I wasn't as sure as she seemed to be.

Both James and I have always hoped that Sarah might one day change her mind and respond to our letters. This is a genuinely selfless wish that goes against our instinct to keep Tom all for ourselves. We want Tom to have some evidence, some scrap of something from her, to show that she cared for him in her own way. We think he'll need this to help him come to terms with the fact that she let him go. If I were in his shoes I would need it, and I know James feels the same. For Daisy it would be the right thing to do, though we have suggested to her that it is possible Sarah is trying to do what she feels is right by leaving Tom to get on with his life. Daisy thought about this and decided that, though a possibility, it didn't make sense. A letter from Sarah, explaining as much, would have been altogether more convincing, would have helped her case, in Daisy's eyes.

But a little piece of us is just like Daisy was last year. And I might as well confess, now that Daisy is being so generous, so level-headed, wise and forward looking, I think that even a once-a-year letter from Sarah to Tom would be an unwelcome interruption to *my* life.

Despite this, Daisy's current view on letterbox contact has reinforced what we believe to be right: like it or not, it would be better for Tom to have the option. I admire Daisy for changing her stance, her opinion, for the good of Tom. That's not to say that Daisy's attitude to the emphasis on adoption has changed. She said to James only a couple of days ago, 'We must never forget Tom was adopted,' but it was followed by the point she wished to make, 'It's very important but he needs to move on too.' I think her quiet dislike of any reminder that Tom is adopted is simply because it gets in the way of them just bundling along together. That oft-repeated question, 'How's he getting on then?' is the chief culprit. Daisy doesn't ask us when this will stop and it appears that our matter-of-fact response that it will fade out is reassurance enough. Had we all been wrong to expect, hope even, that interest would fade just that little bit sooner?

Susan, one of my closest friends, said to me the other day, 'But if you had given birth to Tom I'd be asking the same'. She's right. She would. She's lovely, you see. I tried to explain. I said it was wonderful that she was checking up on me, that she wanted me to know I could talk to her and that she would understand. She told me I had griped once, last year, about people asking after Tom, and she said it had put her off. I apologised and assured her that I needed her and certain others to ask after us because adopting was surprisingly, in some respects, unlike having a birth child, and so a different challenge for us to any we had previously encountered. It felt good to know she realised that, but I didn't want *everybody* to refer to Tom's adoption.

I sat for a moment on my friend's rug surrounded by our playing children, and thought how ridiculous that sounded even though it really was how I felt. What did I want? Everyone else to live by my rules of who could and who couldn't ask? Of course not. I just hadn't thought of it like this before now. Hadn't said it out loud and heard it for what it was: confusing. 'It feels as if Tom has an official title', I told her, although I could see by her face that she wasn't aware of any such thing and so quickly added, 'to some people.'

Daisy has never called Tom anything other than 'Tom' or 'Tommy' – admittedly at varying levels of volume according to the level of provocation, but it has felt at times as if he has walked around under an invisible banner ever since we brought him home: 'Tom, Daisy's Adopted Brother.' So what were people to do? Show no interest? How would we have felt then? I thought about it all the way home from Susan's house.

We had been so open about the adoption in order, ironically, to make it easier for everyone around us, and had then tried hard to preserve a degree of privacy for Tom. In our attempt to move him on from being so recently "adopted" to being an ordinary addition to the family, I had got a little bit muddled.

Once home from Susan's house I blew a big undignified raspberry, slumped down onto a kitchen chair, and made a mental note to myself: In the future, if you can't work it out, how on earth do you expect Daisy to? Or anyone else for that matter? Must do better at figuring things out. Must try harder. I think in trying not to talk about Tom and adoption all the time, I had almost forgotten to talk about him at all with the friends I had pre-Tom. Friends who had seen me through other aspects of my life and who would have been happy to hear me out, to try to understand, and who probably have never, ever seen a banner of any description over Tom's head. Well, maybe just a little one saying, 'Rage Alert,' or 'Here Comes Trouble,' but they've been kind enough not to mention it if they have.

There have been lessons learnt here that will aid us in the future. I've often considered putting an L-plate on Tom's buggy as, despite being a very competent car driver, there have been times it would have been wise for me to have taken out fully comprehensive buggy insurance – I quite possibly rank as one of the most hopeless buggy pushers to ever push a buggy. Perhaps it was also time that I wore an L-plate round my neck. It would at least give people some warning: I'm learning too. I may have adopted, but I am no expert.

What does Daisy think about this? Maybe she's worked it all out and could advise me. Nothing would surprise me less. 'Daisy, do you mind them asking how he's getting on?' and if my gesticulation was anything to go by, "them" was referring to the entire universe. Daisy eyed me warily but didn't seem too fazed by the excessive arm movements and readily accepted another chocolate biscuit.

'I don't mind someone asking, but I'd rather they wouldn't.' She crammed the biscuit into her mouth, munched thoughtfully, and then added, 'Like my friends asking about whether Tom is my real brother'. I swallowed my biscuit. 'Really, they still ask that?' I had truly thought that we had moved on just a little bit further than that. 'Yeah, sometimes,' she raised her eyebrows, 'even though they've asked me before.' I assured her that if it was happening less, then that was progress.

Time was the answer I decided, as with much in life. Tom was still fairly new. In years to come, I believe that his adoption will be incidental. We are slowly getting there. What is more, I have realised that I would rather they asked, that they expressed an interest in our welfare, our happiness, than not. In the future I would do well to remember that.

One thing troubled me in regard to Daisy, and that was the manner in which these questions were being asked. I was interested in the tone used: I hoped desperately that it was not negative. I had no need to worry. 'They're curious but nice,' she said. She understands, you see. Doesn't mean she has to like it. I guess that's exactly how I feel too. I do understand. I need to learn to separate curiosity from earnest interest.

So I've got things wrong along the way. I like to put things right when that's the case, hold my hands up and say 'Whoops!' So Susan, and all you others, 'Whoops!' I need to give everyone else much more time, I can see that. They've had so much less opportunity than us to get their heads around adoption. In the future I will try harder and will encourage Daisy to do the same. Wheel in the proverb: patience is a virtue.

So when Daisy's teacher recently asked each child to bring a treasure box full of precious things that they could discuss in class, I gently offered Tom's adoption certificate and a photo of his adoption day. I suggested that it might be a chance to clear up, with the teacher's help, any lingering confusion for her classmates. I thought it might be a good idea. Daisy didn't agree. 'No. I'll take a photo of him though.' She wanted nothing whatsoever in there to do with his adoption and when I asked why, she simply said: 'He's ours now.'

Of course. Another thought occurred to me. Had I missed something all this time? 'Do you find it embarrassing, Daisy? The fuss and questions about Tom's adoption? The very fact that he is adopted? That Mummy couldn't have another baby?' 'No, it's not embarrassing, Mum. It's different from everybody else. I just don't want to be different.'

I think she's onto something there. Interestingly enough, it was for this very reason that we chose not to attend the adoption support groups after Tom's adoption. But we have ensured that Tom has potential friendships with other children who were themselves adopted and at around the same time as him. I actually met one of our adoption friends through a local support group and then, more than a year later, hooked up with both her and her husband and another couple at the preparation groups. We now see each other on a regular basis, always with the children, and here we talk freely and openly about all our adoption experiences as well as other matters in our lives. And generally we eat a lot of food too. We value their friendship and the sometimes spoken, often not, understanding of all that has passed. Here, insofar as we have all adopted, we are the same as each other, and this will prove important for both Daisy and Tom in the future. The majority of their friends have nothing to do with, no connection with, the world of adoption, and Daisy and Tom may well need to spend time with children who do, ironically, in order to feel "normal".

As well as these regular adoption get-togethers, Tom and I attend a couple of local "stay and play" groups every week with children from all backgrounds and circumstances. By the time he gets to nursery school the children he sees at play-groups will know more about his temper, tears, love for his cousin Annabelle, who goes to the same group, and his big silly grin than anything else about him.

I can relate wholeheartedly to Daisy's desire for normality, especially with so much of the adoption experience still fresh in our minds. I believe that, as long as adopted children feel they are the same as any other child, but also have those reference points to relate their adoption to, there is no need to sit around discussing it to any great extent. If your adopted child is not your first child then you already have a network of people with whom to discuss bedtime and feeding routines, toilet training, behaviour, homework, teenage angst and other parental preoccupations. But it is important to remember that other networks are out there for you to access. As adoption is a life factor and your children's comprehension of adoption changes as your story grows. You never know just when you might want, need, to reach out.

Another thought struck me this morning: support groups are an excellent opportunity to give something back, to offer your experience to others. I attended as a potential adopter who had yet to begin her assessment and found it uplifting, informative and inspiring at a time when so little was happening for us but we already had so many questions. I was matched up with a woman who also had a birth daughter and who had recently adopted. I would not rule out going back some time in the future to return the invaluable support, if and when it feels right for our family.

I suppose Tom is also suffering from "Second Child Syndrome". It comes back to the fact that, though in some respects we have undertaken a different journey with Tom, we have returned to familiar ground, to life pre-adoption, where the family was already up and running.

Our full family diary was one of the reasons that stopped us attending the locally held Adoption Fun Day, which was reportedly brilliant. But the main reason was we simply did not fancy it. That's not to say we are too busy to prioritise adoption, or too flippant about its place in our lives. I would not recommend dismissing this kind of occasion, as it can be a chance to socialise with a whole bunch of people who can empathise with your life as it is now, even more than many of your nearest and dearest. But at the moment, with Tom so young and Daisy so keen on her "normality", it felt right for us to give it a miss. A trip to the park was more up our street. But again, we are grateful to know that such support is there.

Like Daisy, I want the freedom to enjoy today and to deal with things when they happen. But there are future plans in the making regarding Tom. We are thinking through the possibility of having him christened and we only hesitate because neither James nor I are especially religious, in a practising sense at least, though we did have Daisy christened. Alternatively, we are toying with the idea of being mildly less hypocritical and having a naming day. Tom was named by Sarah after children's services persuaded her to gift him something of her own; subsequently, we were encouraged to give him a middle name for the very same reason. We did. In court that day Tom not only became legally ours, but he also acquired a new name.

At some point in the near future we would like to celebrate Tom as a person with our family and friends rather than singling out just the one element of his life. For as time goes by, there is so much more for people to know about him than merely how it was they came to know him.

'We've adopted now, Mum. We're no longer adopting,' Daisy clarified for me as she watched me munch away at the chocolate biscuits, lost in my thoughts. Boy, is she right. Though it may never be a fait accompli, for there is no end date, no finishing line, for a child who is adopted, I do not think it appropriate for either of our children to feel that they are continually undergoing a process, or that they are being watched to see how events unfold. We like them to be content with the here and now. We do not want them thinking too much of the future.

It is important to acknowledge your children's personalities. No child is the same as another and nobody knows your children better than you do. When we embarked on adoption, our birth child was right there at the forefront of our minds; the moment our adopted child came into our lives, we felt that same protectiveness towards him. As with Daisy being first and foremost Daisy, so the only thing special about Tom is being Tom.

To check my theory about children wanting to be allowed to just get on with today, I decided to raise the future with Daisy in regards to Tom being adopted. With the chocolate biscuits safely stashed away for another day, I asked Daisy if she had any thoughts about it – any concerns about what the future might hold.

'You're trying to find out my worries, Mum? I haven't any worries,' and then she added as if it were neither here nor there, 'Not about adoption anyway, and not about the future.' Which brought me right back to the here and now. Our cosy little adoption chat was over.

'So what are you worrying about then?' I waded in. And then I thought, that's just it, that is the most important thing to take from all of this: adoption is an interesting, fascinating, absolutely vital part of our make-up as a family, but it is not our be all and end all. Some things are bigger than the way in which we had our second child.

As for what was worrying Daisy, I headed off to find out. Well, I attempted to, but extracting myself from Tom's vice-like grip on my legs proved almost as great a challenge as adopting him in the first place. Attempting to move across the room in pursuit of Daisy, Tom still attached and chortling away to himself, my money was on school friends. It has featured, almost without challenge, as Number One in our house on our Top Ten Worries list. With Tom delighting in his newly discovered game, I decided to take his approach and make my interrogation fun.

'Daisy, where do you think adoption would come in Top Ten Worries?' I had her attention again. 'About eight,' she replied after a little thought. I was silently relieved as I had been expecting it to come in somewhere around there. 'Daisy,' I said slyly, knowing full well that she could see right through my shamelessly transparent tactics, 'what's at Number One?' By the look on her face, I thought maybe another cup of tea and perhaps another biscuit were in order: for me, not her. I just wanted to help. That's what mums tend to want to do. Whether the issue be adoption or school, as long as children know that their parent, or parents, are open to discussion, then most matters can be addressed, talked through and processed – often instinctively, sometimes with outside advice and support. And as is often the case with children, these things tend to come to the surface when least expected, when you are most preoccupied.

Remember Daisy, the rare occasion your mother summoned up the willpower to spring-clean the entire three-storey house? Perhaps it was the shock that prompted you to disclose your worries that day. Or the family christening over a hundred miles from home, when we spent the happy occasion in tears in the church toilet, and even now, Daisy, when you are being quizzed for your pearls of wisdom and the good of your mother's book. Daisy's "tummy aches" and "headaches" have never yet been about the adoption; they have been about school and problems with friends. An open door policy is the way forward. Though I don't claim for one minute that we have this down to a fine art either; we have been known to dose Daisy with Calpol before realising a good chat would have been medicine enough. Whoops!

Interesting as the future may be, it looks like both Daisy and I have got our hands full with today. With Tom attached to me like some crazed, grinning koala bear, I wasn't going anywhere. Sometimes there really is no time like the present. 'Come tell your old mum all about it,' I said. And I'm glad to say she did.

9

My family and other folk

One of the first things we were asked to do for our assessment was to draw up an eco map – a diagram which clearly showed our relationships and links with family and friends, so that children's services could examine our support network. It did not disappoint then, and it does not now. The people Daisy knows and trusts have played a significant part in how adoption did and did not affect her life.

There is one thing I need to make clear at the beginning of this chapter: I love our family at large and I like our many friends, and value their input and emotional investment. Without them, in particular my parents, my mother- and father-in-law and our brothers and sisters, life would not be what it is today. And so it is chiefly to them that I say, 'Hold on to that thought when you read what follows'.

Watching our family fall head over heels in love with Tom has been a true joy. Barely an eyebrow was raised when we first announced our intention to adopt. Naturally they had some questions too, but the right information allayed any valid and very genuine concerns. My parents had themselves, at a much earlier stage of their lives, considered adopting and had decided that it would not be the right thing to do because they believed that their own parents would be unable to treat and to love the adopted grandchild the same as they did my brother and me. My mum went on to have my little sister, who has listened to me endlessly throughout our adoption process and often felt more like a big sister.

My parents were absolutely right to make this decision, for support to hopeful adopters can be integral to success. They have surpassed themselves as adoptive grandparents, as have James' parents, and although we are gracing them with their adoptive title, they have played their role as grandparents instinctively. They do not see their relationship with Tom any differently to the one they have with Daisy. The four of them will leave Tom, as they will Daisy, a legacy of love and memories. Acceptance was never in doubt. Though they, like us, could only hope for as much, as the leap of faith is for all those caught up in your decision to adopt, not just yourselves.

Childhood sweethearts that we were, I have known James' side of our family for eighteen years. His sister, Kate, was only nine when I first met her and, at that time, attended the school that Daisy now enjoys. I remember her sitting on the sofa with me, during one of my visits in the first few months of our relationship, openly quizzing me on my dental brace with all the rapturous fascination her age group tend to show for the gruesome. I feel as protective towards her as I do my own sister. James' brother, Dominic, was a slightly shy thirteen-year-old, immensely likeable with a winning smile. Like myself, he was the middle child, and though he may never have known it, I liked to stick up for him wherever possible out of shameless, sheer solidarity. I am incredibly fond of them both, as I am of their now long-term partners. His parents, well, they were tipsy the first time I met them but it was

Christmas, and it put me at ease; they are very, very special to me. James' family are my second set and I am lucky to have them. What is more, they love my children.

But the Waltons we are not. Anyway, how boring would that be? I can't write this book or do Daisy justice if I am not able to be honest. No, we tend to nestle somewhere between John Boy's lot and the Colbys from *Dynasty*. Sometimes we tread on each others' feet, sometimes we put our feet in to "it", whatever it may happen to be, at all sorts of inopportune moments, and sometimes, well, sometimes I guess we're just plain grouchy. We have even been known, and I think they'll join me on this one, to get it wrong occasionally. I know. Shocking!

I have chosen to include this chapter because it highlights the intensity of adoption, the impact others can have and, of course, how your decision can in turn impact on the lives of those close to you. Here, I am raising the question of timing: when to bring your child home to live. I think our Walton-Colby clan's mistakes could turn into someone else's "one to avoid" list. By describing what turned out to be the most difficult consequence of bringing Tom home to live with us at the time we did, I hope to heighten awareness of issues that seem small, and very manageable, in comparison to the early ones of 'Can we love someone's else's child?' and 'What if it all goes wrong?' Issues such as 'Have we prepared our family and those around us?' and 'What steps have they taken to inform themselves?' and even 'Are there any feelings hidden behind the smiles?' Not forgetting the 'How thick-skinned are we?'

Generally, Christmas is thought to be a difficult time, an emotionally fraught time to move a child to their "forever" home, and social workers tend to be wary and actively avoid doing so. And they are right. Yet it was deemed best by all concerned, due to Tom's young age, that he be at home with us for his first Christmas. More important than that was the fact that ideally they wanted him placed before he was nine months old, as there is a belief that a child bonds more readily before that age and that cautiousness, clinginess and "stranger danger" kick in thereafter. They had done well by Tom: six months old when our match was approved, when we met him and when we brought him home in time for Christmas. But time was the driver, and the social workers had to work very hard to make it.

Naturally we were delighted and incredibly eager for it to happen this way. It really did seem perfect. For Tom, as for us, it remains to this day very special that his first Christmas was with his forever family. But perfect it was not. Chosen in part for the tight knit family we had been all those years, we fell apart that first Christmas with Tom. It was not the adoption itself that caused the fall-out, but rather a lack of understanding of what we had been through to achieve it that led to an escalation of misunderstanding.

It is the lesson learnt that I wish to explore – not the tit for tat itself because, let's face it, it was Christmas, we were all turkeyed out and we were all tired. But it took months and months for people who loved one another to get back on track. And probably at the heart of it all, in a most unforeseen way, lay the adoption.

The big build-up to that Christmas, not unlike a Hollywood blockbuster, had always run the risk of being over-hyped, and though we four settled in together beautifully, external forces saw us running for the hills. The billed "Daisy's Best Christmas Ever" came crashing down around her and was a flop, to say the least.

I asked Daisy what she remembers feeling about the run-up to that Christmas. 'Nervous,' she answered, 'it was his first ever Christmas. His first ever with us too. It was the first big thing we did together as a family.' James and I had done our fair share of chattering away excitedly and expectantly to Daisy about what a special Christmas it was to be. It started a little flatly on Christmas Eve.

Friends, themselves parents of a baby only weeks older than Tom, who had been in our social circle for as long as James and I had been together, and who knew how long we had struggled to have another child, quite unexpectedly opted out of celebrating Tom's arrival. We received not even a card – the very least we tend to do to welcome all new arrivals – because, they told mutual friends, 'It wasn't the same as having a baby'. We never give gifts in order to receive, but having only recently given their new addition a welcome gift, it would also have been the norm to have bought, or even made, Tom a little something: a token gesture.

Apparently Tom's arrival did not warrant a welcome. Furthermore, the first time they met him, at a friend's gathering that Christmas Eve, the male friend who was holding his own child completely ignored Tom. Never referred to him once. We had quite genuinely expected them to come over to us and apologise for not sending a card; instead, the female friend handed over a Christmas card and barely gave Tom, there in my arms, more than a passing mention. But it transpired that they had managed to take the time to voice their opinions to others, who felt it necessary to explain to us the seemingly rude, quite strange and certainly unexpected absence of warm wishes.

I often tell Daisy something my mother would say to me as I was growing up: 'If you can't say anything nice, don't say anything at all,' and though I mean this as an example for her to live by, I do sometimes wonder how they could possibly not have had something, anything, nice to say to a little boy who deserved it so much. We were completely taken aback. It was understated, yes, back-handed, maybe, but nevertheless a negative reaction to our son. They were our friends. We hoped they had been misunderstood.

We later had a lengthy and very friendly chat; they assured us that indeed there must have been some misunderstanding. They did confess that they had got a little confused as to whether they should send a new baby or an adoption card. We surmised that they had been unable to come to any conclusion. A hundred or so other people who sent new baby or adoption greetings, or cards left blank for the sender's own message had not found it so difficult.

Daisy noticed and was cross that her parents' friends, with whom she had felt so at ease in the past, thought the baby brother she loved so dearly didn't count. The baby brother who had been through so much already in his short life didn't even herald a "hello". I wanted to show her that getting wound up and fighting her corner, Tom's corner, was not the way. I did not want her defending him, us, for the rest of her life. My message to Daisy was to rise above it – something she has done better than I have managed to do.

Sadly, Christmas Day, hectic but fun until late afternoon, deteriorated rapidly, and by the end of it James and I were sitting on our sofa, both trying to say something, anything, to make sense of what had gone so wrong. Right then, home didn't feel like the place we had thought it to be. Daisy had gone to bed confused and worried; Tom was fast asleep, wiped out by his very excitable day and late night; and Christmas special after Christmas special played out on the television. Who needed the ratings war when we had our own primetime bust-up? Where had all that goodwill gone? It was absent in places we had expected to find it and I think that was what affected us the most. We had not been prepared for the unexpected.

We had argued with James' family because they were not happy about the amount of time we spent with them. I think it is safe to say that they had overlooked the fact that we lived on the same road as his parents and had done so for almost four years. With both James' brother and sister living further afield, we were the available local ones, so that in reality we were *always* seeing James' family in one way or another.

But in spite of spending Christmas Day afternoon and early evening with them – even stopping to bathe Tom at their home for all to enjoy – and being ready to see them another day during the Christmas period, it was not enough for them. Yet what *we* really needed was to spend more time alone; we needed to be left to bond, and our reluctance to give up any more of this important time – bearing in mind that this was James's first time off with Tom since returning to work and Daisy's first holiday with him – did not go down very well. As is the way with families, the mud flew when, after taking the children home, James returned to his parent's house to address matters. Unfortunately for all, too much was said. And it would take a long time for feelings to subside. We were too battered and weary to handle it well and were feeling understandably defensive.

Daisy walked past my study yesterday afternoon and I called out to her, 'What do you remember about what happened on Christmas Day last year?' She popped her head back round the door, 'Dad got really upset.' 'He did, didn't he?' I remember how galled he had been, how red his eyes were when he came back down the road to kiss Daisy goodnight. 'How did that make you feel?' 'Disappointed,' she answered, nodding to herself, 'because our first Christmas with Tom went all wrong.' It did. There's no arguing with that. No dressing it up. And she was clear about one thing: a family arguing and falling out over wanting to see each other was quite simply, 'A stupid thing to argue about. You were all arguing about wanting to see each other and then didn't see each other for months after. Stupid.' Takes me back to the beginning of this book when I recall writing, 'Out of the mouths of babes...'

So Christmas had unexpectedly stung. It was my first

Christmas with the son I had waited six years for and for Daisy it was a far cry from anything she had hoped for or been led to expect. And what's more, it seemed to have very little to do with the children. Suddenly it was all about the adults.

We did all finally reunite some eleven months later. We had missed them all. We started spending time again with James' parents a couple of months into the New Year, but it took longer to mend relations with James' sister and brother. Finally, on the occasion of Grandad's birthday in November, all of us got together just like we had that Christmas Day. Not far off from the following Christmas. Daisy says she felt, 'Nervous. I was nervous of seeing them all together again.'

So our first year with Tom was largely spent working on strained relations with James' family when it should never have been about that. I spent twelve months waiting for the next Christmas, as keenly as any child, determined to create the one we should have had. It felt like a long time to me, and so for Daisy it must have been an age. Thankfully, Daisy and Tom's second Christmas together was wonderful from start to finish and allowed us more quality time as a family of four. We opened up our new home and spent Christmas Eve very happily in the company of James' family; we visited my family on Christmas Day morning, before returning home to unwrap toy after toy and watch *The Gruffalo* on television. On Boxing Day we had friends and their girls round for a meal and more of the same. All in all, we safely put to rest the ghosts of Christmas past.

I am sure James' family would prefer that I had not included any of this and I know they regret the episode as much as we do, but leaving it out would have been to ignore one of our greatest learning curves. Introductions aside, it was the most upsetting memory of adoption for Daisy.

I do think the problem was us. We hadn't wanted to weigh our family and friends down with the nitty gritty of our adoption experience. We hadn't talked very much at all about how hard it had been in those introductions and hadn't made it clear or even let it be seen how very tired we were. If we had communicated better then they may well have had a better understanding, and for that I am sorry. Instead, we soldiered on and it must have seemed as if we were on top of the world.

And my family possibly had more of an understanding on how it had been for us, how we were feeling, because I tend to chat more often to them and in all probability James didn't communicate as freely as (not that I wish to generalise but I'm going to anyway) is the way with so many men. I'm sure with hindsight, James's family wish they had supported us to have the time we needed on our own. Their bonding with Tom could have waited; should have waited. In sharing Tom with the extended family so readily and so early, we made a mistake. We should have been more selfish and kept him all for ourselves: Tom deserved that and so did Daisy.

Also, and I think this is hugely significant, James and I felt so honoured to be chosen for Tom that we dared not utter a word of complaint along the way. We knew we were lucky, and to make demands, to batten down those hatches, didn't seem right at the time. Quite obviously we should have had Christmas at home that year and perhaps seen very little of anyone else but that wouldn't have been normal for Daisy, and we did want to see our families. We had wanted to please everyone and ended up pleasing very few. We will always be glad and grateful that we had the privilege of seeing Tom have his first Christmas at home, but I can fully understand social workers' reluctance to make a placement so close to this time of year.

Christmas aside, I wanted to talk to Daisy about the more positive aspects of our family for there are many more of those. 'How do you think your grandparents, aunties and uncles got used to Tom?'

'They just got on with it. He was a new baby. I don't think they thought much about him being adopted.'

I would say that was a reasonable evaluation. 'OK, so how do you feel about sharing them all with Tom?' Daisy adores her grandparents, aunts and uncles and I wondered, though I had monitored it as we went along, how she felt now that there was another little person on the scene stealing the limelight. To be fair to Daisy, she has shared them wholeheartedly with her beloved two-and a-half-year-old cousin, Annabelle.

'Fine. It's normal. Other people have cousins and brothers and sisters. It didn't make any difference.'

'What, even though he spends more time with them and sees them when you're at school?' I was pushing her a little.

'I'm just pleased to have him. I'd rather visit them than go to school of course. No, actually,' another thought had occurred to her, 'everyone else is at school and I'd rather be doing what my friends are doing. It's nice to have a break from him anyway.' Now that sounds more like the healthy attitude I was hoping for; well, attitude, at least.

So overall, Daisy has a very positive impression of how our family welcomed Tom. I think she would say the same of our friends. There were some very touching moments that will stay with us always and some relationships were sealed, we hope, for a lifetime with people who surpassed themselves and helped to ensure that Tom had a warm, nurturing and fresh start in life.

Through adopting Tom we have encountered far more good in our family and in those other folk we share our patch with, than anything to the contrary, and it has been an uplifting experience. Of course, there were not just family and friends involved in our family-making shenanigans – there were the professionals as well. And it is here that we have been so very pleasantly surprised. Aggie,

Jo, Jane and the other social workers we met along the way, including Sue who happened to live just down the road from us, were everything we could have wanted them to be: friendly, caring, with a sense of humour and professional to the last. They were our familiar faces from the system, but there were others who also made it good for us, but most importantly for Daisy.

When the letter came to inform us of our date in court, it omitted to mention Daisy. More as a precaution to ensure they were expecting her and because she had asked to see the invitation and I knew she'd notice, I rang them to confirm that they knew Tom had a big sister. It was only a few days later that I came home to a very official letter addressed to Daisy Belle c/o Mummy and Daddy. Inside was a new invitation with her name on it and her very own letter.

Dear Daisy,

Re Case Number _____

In the Matter of the Adoption and Children Act 2002 And in the matter of Tom _____ , a child.

I know that you and your Mummy and Daddy and your little brother Tom have a very special day coming up and wanted to send you a very special invitation to make sure that you came along too.

Being a big sister is a very special job and we are very sorry that the invitation did not have your name on it before.

We cannot wait to see you, Mummy, Daddy and Tom on 29th June. It will be a very exciting day.

Tell Mummy and Daddy to bring a camera and maybe you will be able to sit in the Judge's chair and have your photo taken.
See you soon!

This letter, for us, transformed the judicial system into the story of Daisy and her "baby bother". With a date and invitation secured, I then wrote to Mrs Bray, Daisy's head teacher, to ask permission for a day's holiday so that Daisy could join the party after the court proceedings. We knew full well that Mrs Bray would want Daisy to be part of it all but sometimes, sometimes you have to go out there and make it happen. So this is what I wrote:

Dear Mrs Bray,

RE: Daisy Belle/VIP

On Saturday we received notice, from the designated Adoption Judge and the Children's Guardian of Tom's Final Adoption Hearing, which will be held on Monday 29th June at 10am.

This is a celebratory final event with the judge in full "costume" and is very much for the children of the family so that they are left with a positive image, after all the officialdom and some substantial stress, of the adoption process. It is when Tom will legally become a Belle. We have invited family and some friends to join us and it is so important to us that Daisy be key in this event.

Would it be possible to keep Daisy out of school on this day please? I'll be honest and say that the actual court appearance will be over and done with before lunch time, if it is not delayed, but we are gathering back at our house for a cheeky glass of bubbles and a toast to celebrate (and Daisy will be in her finery). So I would be very grateful if we could keep hold of her for the whole school day.

To which Mrs Bray sent the following reply:

Dear Mrs Belle

Many thanks for your letter about the adoption meeting for Tom on June 29th and the guest of honour.

I have every pleasure in allowing Daisy to spend the day with you.

May I pass on my best wishes to you and all of your family for a lovely day and a happy life together.

Mrs Bray is the sort of head teacher who, within days of taking up her post as the new head, appeared to know the name of every pupil who attended, and greeted them all personally as they walked in through the gate in the morning. We like her. What's more, the school went the extra mile and in the week that we brought Tom home it just so happened that Daisy received her "well done" certificate in assembly for some piece of work I fail to recall. Coincidence, we don't think. The school was superb both in the run up to Tom and after his arrival, which played its part in helping us settle in together. It gave Daisy respite from the changes at home and a place to go that hadn't changed: a place that celebrated her.

'Daisy, what about the especially nice things other people have done? What stands out about it in your mind?' I wondered which story she would come out with, but all she said was, 'It's when they all treat him just like me'. Just like they should, her tone of voice seemed to be saying.

And so on 29 June 2009 we took one of the largest gatherings of friends and family the judge had seen into a little courtroom in the city to be part of our moment. Admittedly, not all of those we had invited could make it. Nevertheless, it was the fitting, uplifting end to all the formality, waiting and protocol that Daisy had endured. Our aim was to make that courtroom ours. If our two children had to go to court to be joined as sister and brother, then we wanted it to be a child-friendly and very special occasion for them. It was certainly very informal, very friendly – and very quick. The culmination of all we had been through was a brief, painless, "blink and you'll miss it" moment. We were done.

The certificate itself was a rather tin-pot affair and I'm sure Daisy could have run off a better one. But after removing the red ribbon and unfurling it, I struggled to read it aloud to my dad – who simply adores Tom and all the opportunities he brings to buy toy cars and more toy cars – because seeing it in print choked me more than I can say. Tom Dylan Belle was adopted. What's more it was us, Daisy and her mum and dad, with a little help from some rather special people, who had gone and done it. And so our happy entourage streamed past people waiting outside the courts for an altogether different sort of court appearance, but even they smiled at us as we went, and we all headed home to drink champagne in the sunshine: not advisable, but wonderful.

I wondered what Daisy had made of it. 'How did you feel about court?' Her first comment was that her best friend, Holly, and her big sister, Hannah, whom Daisy adores, were unable to be there. 'They were at school.'

'Yes, but how did it feel being there that day?'

'It felt sad,' she said simply.

Sad? That wasn't the answer I had been hoping for but she continued, 'It was the end of our time in our old house; our last special occasion there. I was also excited because Tom was properly ours.' And the way she said this suggested that she had always been his: that she had not needed a judge to tell her but was gracious enough to allow him to feel he could. Being only six years old, she did tag on, 'but I was more excited about moving!' However, she did sit in the judge's chair, though she declined his offer to try on his wig. I still don't know whether it was the possibility of nits that put her off, the fact that it would mess up her "party" hair or that she was embarrassed by a grown-up trying so hard to be fun. I was more than tempted, I have to say.

Afterwards, as Aggie and Jo said their goodbyes, cards were exchanged and Daisy was given one of her own from Aggie. There were a few teary eyes and polite but firm hugs. We will never forget them. They have ensured themselves a welcome in our family for ever after. Daisy opened her card and on the front it said:

> *Here's sending you a little sunshine, a little love, a little kitten, a little hug, a little flower, a little kiss, a little sparkle, a magic wish.*

On the back was written:

> *Dear Daisy...because you are such a great big sister! Love Aggie*

Nothing at all like the portrayal of social workers by the media. In our case they had been thorough, honest, helpful and real. It is a pleasure to be able to write so heartfelt a tribute to the key people in the key institutions that we passed through en route to Tom.

If I could have cushioned Daisy from the more negative aspects of adoption I would have. I would have used bubble wrap around the cotton wool if I could have. Yet I really believe it has done her nothing but good in the long run, for she has grown as a person, though sadly not in height – 'Your time will come, Squirt.' And she knows a little more of what it is like to be human, and at the very least she knows for sure that we, her parents, are only that. There's nothing wrong with falling off the pedestal now and again as long as you get right back up there and show them you are trying.

I know that if anyone had been there in our home and seen Daisy's tears for Tom during the introduction week, if they had seen her trying to befriend Sam, the foster carer's son, or heard her daddy's shameless sobs from the kitchen on bringing Tom home, or if they too had seen her brother for the first time as they stood unwelcome in a stranger's house, then they would know Daisy has seen all this and more. If the other people in our lives had felt just a bit of Cheryl's and Sam's heartache, their very real grief at losing Tom, if they had watched me as I stood and rocked Tom as he cried and stared wild-eyed round the unfamiliar bedroom in the middle of those first few nights, knowing he had no reason to trust me, and then if they had seen him finally give in and take comfort, and if they had felt even a bit of how that made me feel, then they would know only a little of what Daisy knows. If they knew how exposed we were throughout the process, if they understood how daunting the whole scenario had been from beginning to end and what a leap of faith we had taken, then they would understand everything that Daisy has attempted to understand, and all we have tried to guide her through.

Daisy has watched me adjust as Tom took his time to bond with me and has continually told me how she knows he loves me, whilst she waited for him, willed him, not to let her down. And now it breaks my heart to see her delight in just how much of a mummy's boy he has become. Part of Daisy, the bit that is far too grown up, wanted to look after us. She wanted it to work. She has proved herself to be a real team player of whom I am immeasurably proud.

Giving an honest, hopefully insightful and open account of our very personal life story is not easy. I am usually a very private sort of person. At times I have wished for an airbrush and some soft focus to blur the memory of how we felt, what we have said or done, and not said and done. Thankfully, our family and those around us are good people. Somehow and at times we get it right and at others we get it wrong. We have brought Daisy up, as we are now bringing up Tom, to accept that we all make mistakes; that it's admitting mistakes, being able to face up to them and choosing to do something about it and move on that matters. Accepting all emotions as natural is helpful in dealing with adoption and its knock-on effects. It is how we choose to express them, how we handle them, that changes the outcome.

Daisy herself has recently gone through a phase of being consumed with guilt that she has been thinking and wanting to say some 'bad words Mummy, naughty ones like bloody', when her friends are being mean to her and making her feel sad.

'That,' I assured her, 'is OK, Daisy. We all feel like that at times, it's what you choose to do about it that matters.' I thought hurriedly for an example that would surprise her a little and give her faith in herself, 'Even Nana thinks bad things sometimes,' I told her and I took her round to visit so she could hear Nana confess all, which apparently was reassurance enough. Sorry, Mum, your pedestal wobbled a little but you are still up there. It was a real comfort to Daisy, and now she's not so alone down on the ground looking up. It's done her no apparent harm discovering that her wonderful family is just like her.

Choosing to document moments from our life as it really was, setting in print what we felt and did, moreover choosing to turn our lives temporarily upside down and inside out in order to adopt in the first place, was done in good faith. We were a family – James, Jules and Daisy – and we still are. Only thanks to the process of adoption, it now reads: James, Jules, Daisy and Tom. For us, our little circle is complete, but only because we worked together, clung together, remembering all the while what it was that was so important to us: us.

If there is a family out there like us that finds itself in a similar situation with their very own Daisy hoping for a Tom, I dearly hope that it might be a sort of relief or support that someone else has put into words what it was really like to entrust your whole family into the care of a system. To be responsible and worry that you are being irresponsible.

I close this chapter almost at the point where the four of us pick up our skirt tails – sorry James and Tom, not the image you would wish for, I know – and run off into the sunset; only Daisy will need the toilet and complain that her Nintendo DS needs charging and Tom will drop his Snotrag somewhere and will refuse to go anywhere without "him". So not so much running as stopping and starting, and well, the sunset can't be guaranteed. We live in the United Kingdom after all, but we're off to have some fun trying and we've brought our brollies and wellies along too. See, we really have learnt a thing or two along the way.

And sometimes when it feels as if the world does not understand, you'll be amazed just how understanding a place it can be. My lovely mum, Nana, gave me a card recently with a book she wanted James and me to read concerning a man's attempt to trace his birth family. In it is a quote from TS Elliott:

> *We shall not cease from exploring. And the end of all our exploring will be to arrive where we started and know the place for the first time.*

That is how it is to be a family who adopts. We arrived back after our journey to get Tom and we found ourselves a family once more going about our day-to-day lives, but yet whilst it is still the same it is also very different. Adoption changed us for the better, and it has tested us a little and been kind to us also. Daisy probably does see the world a little differently now but it is still her world, and it is our family and other folk who have helped it feel that way.

A sense of perspective is all-important; it wasn't like we journeyed to the moon, after all. We are not the only ones to have made this journey in order to fulfil that innate desire to be a family. As the Apollo 14 astronaut Edgar D. Mitchell, who made the longest moonwalk in history, was recently quoted, 'We are not alone'. Warts and all, we are more glad of that than we can ever say.

10
What if...?

And so we come to a sort of end to the story of how we three became us four. We are still stepping out into the unknown, for though we are not time travellers, we have had to explore the past, present and future like we have never had to before. Since bringing Tom home that crisp, sunny December morning we, and especially Daisy, have been consumed largely with the here and now. It is springtime again, not our first together; contentment has flourished. It feels as if we are ready for all that is to come, and I mean that not in an armed, defensive sense but in more of a "go with the ebb and flow" way. With all that is behind us, we are free to enjoy the retrospective ponderings of 'What if...' It makes for thought provoking stuff. What if, for example, we had not waited a year for our preparation groups as we did, and had consequently been approved earlier? Would Tom still have been ours? Would Daisy have her "baby bother"? Wouldn't we have been matched with another child? And anyway what, what if Sarah had changed her mind about him?

I realised this was something that I had given little thought to, and no sooner had the thought popped into my mind than I blurted it out to Daisy, 'Just think, you may never have met Tom.' She looked at me as she might if I had picked her up from school in my dressing gown, wearing a pink feather boa, a pair of Daddy's wellington boots and star-shaped sunglasses. Which, just for the record, I have never done. I'm an approved adopter don't you know; not that children's services would be critical of anything like that of course; they are far too open minded nowadays for such value judgements. And it was then that Daisy said quite possibly the best thing I think she could have said to me, 'Why not?'

In a world in which Father Christmas and the Easter Bunny reign supreme, this was a step too far for Daisy's comprehension. Fate, it would seem, ranks higher in her esteem than possibility and though it is indeed possible, it is to her unbelievable that Tom might not have been her brother.

We will handle the future as we have dealt with all that is past. We found it helped a great deal to remind ourselves that we were only ever going to be dealing with our own set of circumstances. One set. We are not scared of the unknown any more, for meeting Tom has taught us much and, as I like to tell Daisy, not unlike the Cowardly Lion from *The Wizard of Oz,* we have earned our courage on our yellow brick road to finding out that there is no wizard. Nobody can do it for you.

By all means read, listen and absorb the myriad of stories and case studies that are out there waiting for you and anything else you feel will help along the way, but never forget you will not be living the amalgamation of all you read and hear. Your family, your adventure, your adoption experience will be in some way, or many ways, different from any other. Let others inform but do not let them dictate your actions. I value the books in this series because they tell it how it is. Mine is a completely biased, totally subjective, hopelessly emotional contribution from a novice adopter and an "on the job learning" sort of mother, and for that I make no apology. We are, after all, talking about my children here. When considering your birth children's need for information and preparation, reference books alone are not enough. Go and hear real people with real stories and you might well find your place among them.

However, there are some directions prospective adopters with children could aim to follow. Daisy and I sat down, complete with refreshments, naturally, for one last chat about just that. 'Daisy, what would have made your experience of adoption a better one?'

Her first answer: 'If Sarah had contact. I know we can't make her but that would be better.' This very adoption-friendly and politically correct reply was like a red flag alert for me: this was definitely the last time I would pick her brains on adoption for anyone else's benefit other than her own.

'OK,' I said slowly, 'that's really lovely and very generous, Daisy, but it's me you're talking to. Give it to me straight. Tell me what if anything could have been better for you. Don't think about anyone else. What about how social workers prepared and supported you?'

It didn't take Daisy long to come up with another answer. 'I really think they could have, should have, told me about Tom a bit before they did. It was really, really quick, Mum. If,' and she repeated, 'if I hadn't wanted Tom I had absolutely no time to do anything about it. That's how it felt.' Though we would have made time if this had been the case, there is absolutely no denying the fact that the speed with which it all finally fell into place could have seemed insane.

'How would you have liked it to have been?' She had never once mentioned any of this before and I was fascinated by her frankness.

'They should have told me sooner and much more.

They should at least have sent me a DVD. All I got was a bad photocopy of a photo about this big,' Daisy squints and holds her thumb and index finger about two inches apart, 'and then a few days later a few colour photos,' and to really make her point she looks at me in what I am sure is *my* "Don't mess me around" face, and adds, 'out of date ones too'. She wasn't finished, but left that hanging in the air for a moment. 'And maybe, maybe I would have liked to have seen a proper photo of Sarah then.'

'You would have? Why?' Though it didn't take a psychologist to come up with all the possible answers, I wanted to hear it from her. 'Because didn't *you* want to know who Tom saw when he was born, you know, when he first opened his eyes?' I found myself sliding into soppy movie mode, hence the fast constricting throat and my "Mummy's not going to cry" smile. 'Yes. Yes,' I managed in the rather silly voice that comes from such effort, 'That would have been better.' I think if she could have, Daisy would have been right there at the birth absorbing all there was to be known about her brother. It was such a lovely wish.

'Really,' I reasoned, regaining composure, 'you are, we are, very lucky. You were there with him almost as early as it was possible to be. He was still so little. He won't remember anything before you came into his life, but you can help him learn about it when he's older, and be there to help him to make sense of it. Besides,' and though I knew it was different I said it anyway, 'most brothers and sisters are not there at the births of their new siblings.' Though I knew full well it wasn't the birth she was concerned with but rather that she wanted to start with an understanding of his day one, to have that shared experience.

Now that she was talking straight from the shoulder, I flashed her a carefree smile so as not to put her off, 'OK, what else could have been done better?'

'I think it was quite good actually.'

'You do?' I changed that to a statement almost an octave higher, 'You do!' I was delighted. Perhaps I could put the tea on, get some washing done, help her with her fractions, maybe even tackle the sculpture that is our ironing pile (an activity usually reserved for highs of domestic conscience brought on after visiting the establishments of other mothers more inclined to such tasks; I continue to remain more of a novelty ironer). 'That's great, Daisy.' But as it happens she'd had another thought or two and fractions really would have been a little easier going.

'Maybe I could have known more about the meetings. What were they all about? I don't even know now.' Oh! Why had she never once raised this before? I knew the answer. I hadn't asked. 'Okey dokey, Daisy...' and I explained that we had operated on a "need to know" basis due to her young age and also according to the level of interest shown by her at each given stage. I let her think about this for a moment. 'Did you feel left out?' A "yes" would have been telling enough but I was very calmly and firmly informed, 'A bit, but you could have stopped that'.

Right. That was me told. 'You're right of course, Daisy, and I'm sorry you felt that way...' 'I did.' 'Yes, but,' (my own mother's "no buts..." went through my head), 'you were younger then.' 'I'm not now,' and her steady eyes met mine.

'Fine,' and I gave her a rounded-up, child-proof summary of all our meetings, interviews and training days – not entirely dissimilar, as it turned out, to a sixty-second Shakespeare play. Finishing with a flourish, I raised an eyebrow as I watched her face for a reaction, reached blindly for my mug of strong tea, and draining it tried to recall if I'd seen a bottle of white cooling in the fridge for later. If I rang James he'd pick one up on the way home. Maybe some chocolate too, or even ice-cream...

Daisy seemed satisfied. How, I thought, can we almost simultaneously be writing messages to the Easter Bunny and be debating the ins and outs of adoption? I decided to use the silence to move things on a little, to make it personal, preferably on to somebody else. 'What did you think about Aggie and Jo then?' James and I feel very protective of our social workers and I wondered now what Daisy had truly made of them.

'Nice'.

That's all?' I stopped chewing the end of my pencil. 'You know you shouldn't do that,' she told me.

'It's my pencil,' I replied hoping she wouldn't notice that it was in fact hers: they all are, only I tend to "acquire" them for my pencil pot on pretence of looking after them for her. 'But you should not chew yours. Very bad for you...'

'Like smoking?'

'Er, yes. Don't do that either.'

'I won't, it's disgusting,'

'So anyway, I get all that "you didn't do this, you didn't do that" stuff and they get "nice"?' She smiled at me and laughed, 'OK, I didn't want strange people coming into my house and asking me things. It was a bit scary. If someone asked me if I wanted them there or not I'd say definitely not.' I'm quite glad I didn't ask before now. I'm quite glad they didn't either.

'I liked the worksheets though, oh and reading *Bridget's taking a long time* and changing all the names to ours. Actually, I ended up really liking my special interview with Aggie too. The one just for me.'

Putting it together, thinking about us: what have we learned from Daisy that we can pass on to other families with children getting ready to adopt?

> **More** child friendly involvement in the assessment process.
>
> **More** discussion of and preparation for the reactions of other people in a child's life.
>
> **More** information about the new sibling sooner. This is a fine balance, I appreciate, as it is in nobody's

interest to raise a child's hopes before a match is possible, and we were unable to tell Daisy about Tom until the day we did – the day he was freed for adoption, just two weeks before the introductions (though officially this should have been three days later, on the day of our matching panel).

An exchange of DVDs and good, current photographs to dispel some of the mystery and foster a sense of familiarity between siblings-to-be.

Adopters having their parental heads on in the planning meeting that takes place before introductions begin. Really think through the arrangements and how they will affect your children already in the family; make them your top priority alongside the adopted child, and make sure what you say is minuted.

More time spent with the adoptive child in the adoptive home during introductions and less time with the foster carer's family.

Foster carers and their children being better prepared for separation and better supported during introductions.

Closer monitoring at every stage of introductions, including birth children's reactions, would avoid misunderstandings and misconceptions.

And what really worked for us?

Making the new sibling as real and as unthreatening as possible throughout the entire process: referring to them as Little One worked for Daisy.

Answering Daisy's questions age-appropriately.

Offering but not pushing any child-friendly material on the subject.

Making the adoption as much Daisy's as ours.

Keeping a sense of humour, or at least recovering it as soon as possible.

Getting on with life, whatever that meant at any given time, so that no time was wasted or resented as a result of adoption. Children should not lose out because their parents are having a trying time producing their brother or sister. Easier said than done, of course, but we did things Daisy still talks about now like boating on the river (laughing until our sides hurt each time as I am almost as bad at rowing as I am with the buggy and James, though better, struggling to go under bridges without ploughing into the sides), picnics anywhere and everywhere, getting Einstein our dog, a few magical days in Disneyland Paris, and putting up a chicken coop for the chickens we ended up cancelling when our moment came! Not that I am advocating any of these in particular, but they gave Daisy highlights to pin her childhood on.

Daisy and Tom's bond was instantaneous, which was a huge joy and relief to us both; it turned out they needed no assistance from us, or time to get going. James' love for Tom grew very earnestly and honestly in the first few weeks into full blown adoration, helped by the fact that Tom was drawn like a magnet to James. Tom tested me and certainly reserved most of his anger and tears for me, which really was rather an honour, though it did not feel that way at times. So OK, Tom's deep rooted bond with me didn't turn on one day like some tap of love, it had to be cultivated before growing and blossoming with trust. I had to earn it, tend to it, was hell bent on it. I had to prove myself to him but he knows now: no matter how cross she may get some days when I chalk on her walls, throw the contents of my bedroom down the stairs, throw the contents of my sister's bedroom down the stairs, roll blue-tack in my hair or swirl the water in the toilet bowl round and round with my hand... this one's for keeps.

Thus I consider myself one of the luckiest mums to have

graced this earth for I have enjoyed a successful pregnancy with Daisy, and whilst I couldn't explain satisfactorily why I wanted another child, I wanted one. I wanted to be a mum again and what was more, I wanted to offer that longing to a child who needed it. Thanks to adoption we found each other.

Adoption is undoubtedly a time for the most serious soul searching we can be asked to do in our lives. To ask a child to undertake it is a huge responsibility. Conception is the most private of human affairs, infertility is a rather mixed bag and adoption is the most public. Daisy is, as are children like her, an invaluable guide for looking at adoption through the eyes of a child. And so today, I asked the silly question again. 'Daisy,' a distant voice from a far off land, I waited for the television glaze to clear from her eyes, 'Daisy, was adopting Tom the right thing to do?' The answer came, flippant, gilded with an edge of "ask a silly question, get a silly answer," in the form of an eloquent, 'Yeah,' before giving way to a familiar, 'He's the best brother in the world,' and then I've lost her again to the remote control. Which Tom then tries to wrestle off her and a tug of war ensues. Not for the first time I have to remind her of his official "Best brother in the world" title, to which she replies with a mere huff and then adds: 'I didn't realise how annoying he would be though'. I laugh as I walk out of the room leaving them to it with 'I did warn you,' and my throat does that boa constrictor thing again because part of my quest was for my children to have one another to fall in and out with. Good old-fashioned sibling rivalry. Or all-out war, depending on the day. It's a beautiful thing.

The ironies of adoption never fail to amuse me; like me screeching at the children last night to leave each other alone and losing sight, for a moment or five, of that "beautiful thing" we had waited so long for. And other more poignant times like just before the final court hearing when we considered the possibility of Sarah changing her mind about letting Tom go. As James had said, 'It would be like sending him to live with strangers.' Our son? Ridiculous, the mere thought of it. Preposterous. And how is this for irony: no amount of assessment would be enough to secure my two a new set of parents.

And there is a greater irony still: would we do it again? And the answer is a resounding 'I don't know'. For we are so happy, so content, that it is not a question of whether we would or would not adopt again but rather whether we wish for a third child. That's not to say we haven't all enjoyed speculation on the subject. Could we love another child as much as we do Daisy and Tom? Our Achilles' heel has always been our unknown infertility, which in a weak moment can play havoc with my "what ifs". Not "what if I had got pregnant after Daisy," because I remain eternally glad that I did not – I cannot imagine my second child being anyone other than Tom. Should we hanker after revisiting either option again, it would be because Daisy and Tom are so wonderful, and not to fill a gap. What is hardest is knowing that there are other Toms out there waiting. It would haunt me forever not to give another child all that should be theirs, in order to pursue a pregnancy, but we cannot let what we have heard, learnt and seen send us off on a lifetime of guilt trips. Adoption services are not so much looking for altruistic types as for people that are right for the children they have in their care; as we must look out for what is right for the children entrusted to us both.

Somehow or other we ended up with one girl and one boy and our contentment will never be taken for granted. That's not to say we haven't debated other possibilities. We have looked into fostering; our own experience made us very seriously consider all we have to offer, but we have concluded that though hard to walk away from it, we fear it would be detrimental to Daisy and Tom. Fostering would introduce them and expose them to an interrupted lifestyle that I would not wish for them, though it pains me a little to say it. In any case, James and Daisy are now dead set against it and both know enough to know their own minds on the matter. One thing adoption has taught me is that no one knows where the future may find us, but right now we're here.

Besides, we have yet to live as a family when Tom becomes aware of his adoption; we have yet to help him through all he may have to cope with, and what disruptions and upsets that may bring to our family, we cannot know.

Daisy's opinion on the matter of whether she would like another brother or sister (and when I say "another", I stress not as a replacement for Tom – she has been very firmly warned off putting him up for auction on eBay) was very clear, very definite. It came as an enthusiastic 'Yes' followed by 'Oh, Tom. Mum! He's just rubbed out my drawing,' then a heavy despairing 'TOMMY!' through gritted teeth. I'm delighted to say she's no advocate for adoption; I don't think she could care less by what means we happened upon another child. Looking at the expression on her face while manoeuvring Tom to a safer distance, right now I wouldn't even say she was an advocate for baby brothers, but somehow the baby boy we were introduced to, the little girl who dreamt of making stink bombs with him, James and I – well, we've done alright by ourselves.

'Really, he's just my brother. I don't know why some people make such a big deal out of it,' Daisy came out with recently and then, as if wrapping it up and telling me my work was done she added, 'and I love him.' She's right. Again. She does. We do. Tom has more love than he probably knows what to do with and as I turn towards my greatest hurdle yet, that ironing pile – which my mother has offered to help me with on more than one occasion, so nervous does it make her to see it – I buzz with pleasure from my head to my toes.

We have discussed from the outset the need to get our

heads round the simple fact that there is no guaranteed happy ending and as this is the place where I draw the line in telling our tale, it is our fairy tale. Someone who had recently given birth said to me once, 'I wish I'd done it your way,' referring to the fact that I hadn't had to go through the trials and tribulations of pregnancy and birth and actually, though it riled me when I thought of how much we and all other adopters have to go through even before being approved as acceptable parents, I am grateful that we were given the chance to do it because it has shown us that life is more marvellous at times than we would otherwise have known.

The message? Have a good old think. Prepare. Be watchful. Involve the existing children in your family as much as possible and be ready to take their criticism later, when they sit you down and list all your oversights. Remain calm(ish). Love them. Do what you already do as a parent. But get on with it.

And I'll tell you what Daisy wouldn't do; she wouldn't write a book about it. She'd deal with each day at face value and look for nothing more. But as British scholar and novelist C.S. Lewis wrote, 'We read to know we are not alone,' and that ultimately is why I have written this book; so that it is there for a parent, like me, of a child, like Daisy, to read.

When Daisy met Tommy something special took place that lends serious weight to the nature versus nurture debate. If the "what ifs" had been greater than the desire to make it work, then there would have been no Daisy and Tom. Now that, never mind a pregnancy, *is* inconceivable.